SELLING GOD'S WAY

Maximize Your
Income and Business
Relationships

MICHAEL HAMER

LUCIDBOOKS

Selling God's Way

Maximize Your Income and Business Relationships

Published by Lucid Books in Houston, TX
www.LucidBooks.com

ISBN: 979-8-90344-400-7 (Paperback)
ISBN: 979-8-90344-023-8 (Hardback)
eISBN: 979-8-90344-024-5

Special Sales: Most Lucid Books titles are available in special quantity discounts. Custom imprinting or excerpting can also be done to fit special needs. Contact Lucid Books at Info@LucidBooks.com

Editorial: Inspira Literary Solutions, Gig Harbor, Washington

"Hamer clearly knows the business of selling. Rich with Scripture verses and biblical principles, this is a book that believers who are in sales will study and refer to often."

—**Bruce K. Bell,** Ph.D.
Past Dean of Liberty University's School of Business

"This is a must-read book for anyone who needs to improve their lot in life...because the greatest teachers sell education, the greatest preachers sell faith and the greatest parents sell their values to their children. Learn to sell from a master teacher who teaches the principles of the real Master Teacher."

—**Willie Jolley,** Best Selling Author of *A Setback Is A Setup For A Comeback* and *An Attitude of Excellence!*

"Selling requires a solid foundation of wisdom and knowledge. Author Michael P. Hamer taps into the world's best source for information, the Bible, and connects us with that resource in a fresh way."

—**Jeff Arnette,** Executive Producer &
Host of *The Arnette Report*

*In loving memory of my mother Amelia Hamer,
father Warren Hamer, grandfather Benjamin Austin,
and great-great-grandmother Nancy Austin.*

*I dedicate this book to my family. I love you all very much.
I pray for God to bless us with an abundance of grace and
mercy, and I pray that we seek to know and do
God's will as we strive to live God's way.*

Table of Contents

Introduction: Faith, Hope, Love 1

Chapter 1: What Is Selling God's Way? 7

Chapter 2: Remain in Jesus 21

Chapter 3: The Sales Process 43

Chapter 4: Committed and Competent 61

Chapter 5: Prospecting 77

Chapter 6: The Questions 105

Chapter 7: Presentations 131

Chapter 8: Closing 157

Chapter 9: Objections 181

Chapter 10: Service 205

Chapter 11: What Not to Do 221

Chapter 12: What to Do 245

Appendix: Seven Characteristics of Powerful Sales Presentations 269

A Seller's Prayer 277

Acknowledgments 281

About the Author 283

Endnotes 285

INTRODUCTION:

Faith, Hope, Love

And now these three remain: faith, hope and love. But the greatest of these is love.

—1 Corinthians 13:13

Faith

Selling God's way will lead you to the best possible results and relationships, but it requires that you faithfully apply biblical wisdom. Whatever way you sell expresses your faith. It reveals your god—that is, what you rely on for significance, security, and success. Everyone has faith in something: When you turn on a water faucet, you have faith that water will come out. When you hand over money to make a purchase, you have faith that your money will be accepted. A person's faith may be in several gods; the god of their career may not be the same god of their social life. At one time, the god I served at work was not the same Lord that I served at home. My god at work was self-serving ambition, while my deity at home was the Bible's God. My work, which was selling advertising, included components of righteousness rooted in biblical principles, but my actions were guided by a desire to accumulate cash, positions, and possessions. I sought status and success using what I had learned from managers and experience. I neglected the ways of God, despite knowing that those time-tested ways contained the power to produce miracles.

I encourage every salesperson to examine their relationship between faith and selling. You may discover, as I did, that your faith as a salesperson lies in a resource or talent, and not the Bible's God. That resource might be one thing or a combination of many things, such as your competitive nature or ability to persuade. Or maybe you put your faith in a set of secular business principles or another person, such as a sales manager. However, if you believe in the Bible's God, then your selling style should be a by-product of your commitment to living righteously, an expression of thanks to God for your personal salvation, and a reasonable act of service considering God's grace and mercy.

I wrote *Selling God's Way* to assist believers in selling God's way by confirming spiritual insights while also improving their information base. If you do not believe in the Bible's God, or if you are not relying on your faith in God while selling, then I beseech you to try selling God's way. He promises to reward those who diligently seek Him.

Hope

At an early age, I learned that an honest person does not intentionally state something false or omit information that could be considered important. Therefore, when I began selling advertising in 1981, my first thought was that this industry desperately needed an honest person because I observed far too many salespeople being dishonest by overstating benefits, manipulating research, and omitting information. My hope for honesty grew into a hunger for righteousness as I observed salespeople across various industries using all types of sin to succeed. I also observed a pervasive atmosphere among companies that treated salespeople unethically. For example, far too many salespeople were hired into positions that delivered less income and upward mobility than they had been led to believe, if not promised, during their interviews.

As I began writing this book, much of the world was mired in an elongated economic nightmare. Home sales suffered because of mortgage companies selling unethical financing. Auto sales decreased as the industry's reputation for using deceit increased. Financial companies made news because of the millions lost by executives who tried to explain their enormous bonuses with nonsensical assertions. Energy companies seemed to specialize in selling an inaccurate picture of their plight as their profits rose into the billions.

Over the years, I became increasingly disheartened by seeing so many salespeople and companies incorporating sin into their business practices to succeed. I wondered whether these people knew they were sinning whenever their sales process included half-truths and things forbidden by God. I wondered whether they knew their sinful lifestyles damaged their relationships with customers. I surmised that many did not understand that any type of sinful lifestyle puts one's fellowship with God and people in jeopardy, possibly constructing a path to ruin rather than heavenly rewards.

The overwhelming presence of wrongdoing in business led me to write this book in hope that I could help salespeople discard sin and embrace righteousness. This hope guided me to incorporate concepts in the book that could lead others to use *Selling God's Way* for more than maximizing revenue and relationships; the purpose of this book is to encourage a greater use of the Bible, which is the world's best book. I hope this book strengthens believers' fellowship with God as it increases the Holy Spirit's power in their lives, and I hope this book will lead nonbelievers to trust God not only for success while selling but also for a far more important thing, which is an eternal life in Heaven after their time in this world ends.

Love

Love provides the power and perseverance to sell successfully and righteously. It motivates you to do things that show what you rely on for significance, security, and success. Your love for God and people will prompt, even propel, you to consistently demonstrate Christ-honoring behavior, even when predicaments and people pressure you to do things that ignore or go against biblical wisdom and righteousness.

You are empowered by believing the promises found in the Bible. These promises equip you to love God and people in ways that allow you to retain or reclaim an abundance of blessings. At the same time, you're being strengthened by an overwhelming sense of gratitude for all that a loving God is doing in your life. Being grateful motivates you to continue living a life pleasing to God and to behave righteously with all people regardless of circumstances, whether you are selling or just interacting with others as you strive to live successfully. Of course, all this is only possible if you connect your faith, hope, and love to God. Also, you must believe that God's personal love letter to you (the Bible) conveys truth and inerrant instructions for daily living, and that His Holy Spirit lives in you as a personal guidance counselor and intimate comforter.

Love birthed this book, and gratitude motivated me to complete this project. I thank God for saving me from the punishment I deserve. All my sins, including my future transgressions, are forgiven. I believe in my heart and can confess with my mouth that Jesus Christ is my Lord and Savior. I believe Jesus Christ suffered a horrific death on the cross for my sins and was brought back to life by God. I am destined to live after death, into eternity with God in Heaven-Paradise. Currently, the Holy Spirit, which Jesus described lives in me, counseling and comforting me as I strive to live according to God's will.

My love of God has matured into an appreciation of the Bible and an acceptance of all people. In the Bible, I find powerful promises of success and salvation. I find ways to meet all my needs. In His people, I find other faithful followers, believers who enrich my life as a by-product of their relationship with God. I also encounter nonbelievers and false followers. The latter group professes to believe in the Bible's God, but their deeds and lifestyles serve Satan or other things not created to lord over any area of one's life. The love I show for believers, nonbelievers, and those who merely profess to believe exhibits and empowers my love for doing things God's way. It is also an expression of gratitude for the grace, mercy, and blessings that I've received because of my God-given faith. My desire is that *Selling God's Way* will help the people I love achieve the best possible sales results, using the Scripture I love, which was given to us by the God I love.

CHAPTER 1:

What Is Selling God's Way?

All Scripture is God-breathed and is useful for teaching, rebuking, correcting, and training in righteousness, so that the servant of God may be thoroughly equipped for every good work.

—2 Timothy 3:16–17

God-Inspired

The year is around AD 67. The Apostle Paul has been arrested again and awaits execution. No other person, except Jesus, has led more people to accept Christianity than Paul. As he awaits execution in a Roman jail cell, Paul writes a letter to Timothy, a Christian leader in Ephesus. Paul reminds him to always rely on Scripture. He tells Timothy that God inspired all Scripture, making it useful for teaching, correcting, rebuking, and training in righteousness.

Even if you do not believe in God, I think you will find it difficult to oppose the ethical principles promoted in the Bible, especially as it relates to human interactions. Being honest, loving, kind, forgiving, and patient with people will always yield satisfying results. Although companies and salespeople embrace various strategies to sell, serve, and satisfy their customers, their most valuable activity is found in each human interaction. Innovation and technological advancements constantly bring about new and different products and services to sell and ways to sell them. Sometimes, economic realities force change in what is being sold and how it is being offered. But regardless of all that occurs with selling a product and service, having a salesperson who is honest, loving, kind, forgiving, and patient with potential buyers will always yield the best results for both seller and buyer.

Martin Luther King Jr said:

> Through our scientific and technological genius, we've made of this world a neighborhood. And now through our moral and ethical commitment, we must make of it a brotherhood. We must all learn to live together as brothers—or we will all perish together as fools.[1]

If a salesperson's actions are rooted in a moral and observable commitment to righteously sell, serve, and satisfy at all points of interaction, then they contribute to a buyer's well-being. This not only creates a satisfied customer, but it may also create a

---

[1]Martin Luther King Jr, "Remaining Awake Through a Great Revolution," delivered at Morehouse College, Atlanta, GA: 1958.

friend and confidant who expresses that satisfaction in future purchases, rousing recommendations, and brand loyalty.

Selling God's Way

Using biblical principles and wisdom to sell is what I call "Selling God's Way." It's applying the Word of God to all aspects of selling, regardless of whom we sell to, what we sell, when we sell, where we sell, why we sell, or how we sell. Throughout this book, I'll use biblical principles and Scripture to address all the major aspects of selling: prospecting, questioning, presenting, closing, objections, and servicing. In the Bible, God gives us an everlasting guide for everything; therefore, the Bible should serve as the final authority for anything sales- or work-related. Biblical wisdom remains useful and valuable forever (see Mark 13:31 and Hebrews 4:12).

Selling God's way means selling righteously. Throughout the Bible, it's clear that righteousness is the character and quality of being correct, or justifiable, from a godly perspective. Throughout this book, I use the word *righteously* to describe the way we should sell. The Bible tells us that the ability to do things righteously should come through faith in Jesus Christ. Although many righteous things we do while selling arise from human traditions and teachings, if we analyze the principles behind those things, we'll see that even these practices are rooted in biblical principles. This includes practices such as fair pricing, accurate research, serving to satisfy, and considering a prospect's needs.

Unfortunately, during trials and temptations, we may consider or even succumb to doing things that directly oppose righteousness. Most salespeople want to succeed righteously.

However, life's worries, the pursuit of riches, and the desire for pleasure often strangle righteous inclinations. Fear of failure, anxiety, and stress can also invade a person's thoughts and emotions, leading them to abandon righteousness. Far too many salespeople fall into sinful selling styles because of anxiety, fear, or evil desires, especially during difficulties. Under the guise of self-protection, some salespeople even abandon being righteous not only with their customers, but also with their managers and upper-level executives. Satan also schemes so that people follow him and forsake God.

However, we must believe that regardless of perceived consequences or predictable outcomes, we will attain the best possible good, because through our personal relationship with Jesus, all our needs will be supplied. Jesus Christ will strengthen us to succeed righteously, if we adhere to His teachings. Jesus showed us how to be righteous through the way He lived and died, demonstrating His love for God and people. Of course, one of my core convictions is that Jesus died and was brought back to life by God; His resurrection made it possible for everyone to become righteous and fruitful regardless of circumstances (see Romans 3:22, 2 Corinthians 5:21, Philippians 4:13, and Philippians 4:19).

What follows are examples of three companies I found selling righteously in 2022. These companies are committed to following principles and processes rooted in biblical morality:

- *Inspire Investing*, a company founded by Robert Netzly; it manages billions of dollars. Inspire has a passion for investing in companies not only based on financial wisdom, but also on their moral perspective. This leads them to select investment opportunities not only based upon a company's financial statements, but also their moral responsiveness and acts of righteousness as well. Additionally, Inspire Investing donates more than 50 percent of their net profits to ministries.

- *ServiceMaster Brands*, a leader in needs-based services for nearly a century. Their nine brands serve homes and businesses each year in the restoration, cleaning, moving, bioremediation, and property inspection.

  The company was founded by the former minor league baseball player Marion E. Wade, who opened a mothproofing business in 1929. After recovering from temporary blindness caused by a chemical accident in 1945, Wade was inspired to create a company that viewed "each employee and customer as being made in God's image—worthy of dignity and respect."[1] Theodore Malloch, author of *Spiritual Enterprise: Doing Virtuous Business*, says that ServiceMaster is an example of servant leadership. As of 2023, the company is home to over 3,500 franchisees across more than 4,900 locations, serving over one million homes and businesses each year. ServiceMaster does business under nine brands across fifty states and nine countries; it generates more than $3.5 billion in systemwide sales.

- *Tyson Foods, Inc.*, the world's largest chicken company. It has a dynamic culture built on faith and righteousness. Here is a statement from the company's founder John Tyson: "From the beginning, our company has been built on faith, family, and hard work. That tradition,

> our core values, and 'doing what's right' are deeply embedded in our culture."[2]
>
> The company's culture is prominently displayed on its website and is well known for their employees' behavior. The website lists "five Cs" as its cornerstones: Caring, Candor, Creativity, Collaboration, and Commitment.

I mention these companies because they seem to have developed an all-encompassing cover of peace and joy through using biblical righteousness as a foundation for selling and conducting business.

Apply Always

Using biblical principles and Scripture to sell is what I call selling God's way. It's applying the Word of God to all aspects of selling, regardless of whom we sell to, what we sell, when we sell, where we sell, why we sell, or how we sell.

Unrighteousness: Sin

Temporal values, a craving or greed for things we see and pride in our position and possessions, can entrap us in unrighteous behavior in the sales process to gain income, status, or recognition. We may be subconsciously motivated to do unrighteous things while selling to avoid a myriad of fear-based consequences, from the loss of a paycheck to the loss of a parking space. Stress and self-serving ambitions can also lead us down the path of selling unrighteously, which may end in significant loss or unnecessary setbacks. Here are examples of three companies that were caught up in unrighteousness and its consequences:

- *Wells Fargo Bank*, one of the largest and most profitable banks in the United States. In 2016 Wells Fargo paid over $180 million in fines for opening accounts and credit cards their customers never requested. The total number of these fraudulent transactions was well over a million. The unrighteous motivations that led to this ungodly behavior appear to have affected more than five thousand of the bank's employees, from the CEO to lower-level managers and salespeople attempting to achieve demanding and unrealistic sales goals. The Wells Fargo CEO eventually resigned, and five thousand of the bank's employees were fired because of this scandal.
- *Mylan*, a global pharmaceutical company, was supposedly committed to setting new standards in healthcare. In 2016, the company paid over $460 million in a settlement with the US Justice Department for the EpiPen fiasco. (The EpiPen device administers epinephrine to those suffering from anaphylactic shock following an allergic reaction.) Mylan increased the price by 400 percent over a ten-year period. In 2016, the CEO received a $98 million pay package. Unfortunately, during this same ten-year period, the cost of paying for this lifesaving drug became challenging and at times painful for many American families, especially those with high-deductible health insurance.

Due to the bad publicity from the settlement for price gouging and a lack of compassion, Mylan's stock dropped drastically. In June 2017, a report by the Institutional Shareholder Services excoriated Mylan for the "outsized compensation" of its directors. The report urged Mylan's shareholders to "oust all existing directors."

- *ITT Tech* was one of the largest for-profit educators in the US before it closed in September 2016. Founded in 1969, ITT Tech grew to 130 campuses in thirty-eight states. After ongoing accusations of fraud, deceptive marketing, and harassing students, federal and state authorities began investigations. In 1998, an ITT Tech whistleblower reported on the school's use of predatory recruitment practices. In 2004, federal agents raided campuses in ten states. Finally, in August 2016, the United States Department of Education prevented students from using federally guaranteed student loans at ITT Tech locations; subsequently, all ITT Tech campuses were closed, and ITT Tech filed for bankruptcy.

I share these three examples not to condemn any of these people and organizations, but to point out the prevalence of sin in far too many selling arenas. I also want to point out the consequences of these deeds, especially when brought into the light and made known publicly. Millions of dollars lost, reputations damaged, character crises, and company closings are just some of the consequences from people selling in ways that go against godly wisdom. People experience all types of setbacks and stress whenever they or their company sell unrighteously. All these examples are taken from just one year. I could have written a complete book of all the occurrences in the last five years. I highlighted incidents in the banking, healthcare, and educational industries, but in my research, I found examples across all industries of people who appear to be committed to doing unrighteous things while selling.

I use examples from these three industries because people often approach companies in these industries in distress, seeking desperately needed help such as financial guidance, medication, and education. So, we would hope that any thought of unethical or immoral behavior in selling to these prospects would be far from the hearts and minds of most business executives.

What's desperately needed now and what I am optimistic about is that the people involved in these situations are claiming responsibility for their roles in these tragedies, confessing their sins, and repenting for this type of behavior. Regrettably, at times, it takes painful predicaments to bring about change within a person, but thankfully, these types of changes do happen, halting sin and destruction and resurrecting righteousness. Ideally, all who are involved in these situations learn to sell with a conviction and set of principles firmly rooted in God's Word, with His idea of what's right and wrong. Hopefully, more people will rely on the teaching of Jesus Christ and the guidance of the Holy Spirit to satisfy their yearnings as they set goals and implement selling strategies. Prayerfully, their attitudes and actions will reflect a heart and mindset that strives to love and serve God and people, much like Jesus Christ did.

My Sales Career

Looking back over my sales career, I see where income and relationships suffered because of decisions I made that were not righteous, Christ-centered, or Bible-based—until a time came when my life unraveled and I needed to reexamine everything. At that time, I began to go through ordeals in which I experienced complete brokenness in every area of my life: home, health, career, finances, and even friendships. My sales job required me to work with people who sought my demise. Mired in a terrible divorce, I spent almost three months in a hospital bed, near death because of a bacterial infection.

In my turbulence, I sought God for deliverance. I was searching for a way to stop the pain, a way to unhook from the physical, emotional, and mental anguish brought on by my sins and the schemes of Satan. I was seeking restoration, resolutions, and reconciliation in almost every area of my life. As I lay in that hospital bed, God gave me the inspiration to write this book. In that same year, I joined a Bible-teaching church that ignited my spiritual growth. I started using the Bible as the final authority for everything. By seeking a deeper relationship with God, I discovered that my best success came whenever the Bible served as an instruction book for decisions regarding anything.

Useful and Valuable Forever

Through seeking God, I discovered that my best success came whenever the Bible served as an instruction book for decisions regarding everything. Biblical wisdom is always useful and valuable.

I left the hospital committed to selling precisely as the Bible instructed. I began using a Bible concordance to gain a godly perspective on traditional aspects of selling such as prospecting, questioning, closing, objections, and servicing. In my search, I discovered the Bible's first sales transaction in the book of Genesis: an exchange of stew for a birthright between twin brothers Esau and Jacob. In seeking to become a better prospector, I discovered a correlation between Jesus's parable about the wise and foolish builders and salespeople attempting to build a clientele. Today, I strongly recommend using the principles of the wise builder that Jesus outlined when prospecting for customers.

Before my brokenness and epiphany, I put my faith in secular sources to sell successfully. I read dozens of business books, conversed with countless sales pros, and hounded sales managers for their success secrets. My method of preparing for sales calls included listening to recordings by nationally renowned sales experts while driving to appointments. My employers hired some of the most prestigious sales consultants in the country to help me and my coworkers sell more. They often instructed us to sell to prospects who at best marginally needed what we offered and to trust in our own ability to make sales. However, in reviewing my results, I realized that any selling guidance not connected to biblical wisdom yielded inferior and sometimes harmful results.

Today, I thank God for any success. This gratitude was not always part of my past because I attributed much of my success in selling to my own abilities. I was unaware of how much God gifted and loved me until after my brokenness and near-death experience. The combination of my personal tragedies and my Christian upbringing in Indiana led me into a deeper commitment and relationship with Jesus Christ, the church, and Bible study. Now, without any doubts or apprehensions, I know it's only through God's grace and mercy that I'm able to accomplish anything worthwhile, especially during challenging circumstances. The following are examples of how God blessed me:

- In 1988, I sold almost two million dollars of advertising time at a beautiful music radio station in Washington, DC. As of 2023, few salespeople in that market have come close to selling that much radio advertising.
- In 1993, after my first year in the cable TV industry, Kevin Smith, the vice president and general manager of the station, wrote this tribute to my accomplishments: "Michael has been with our company for a year now, and his sales team led the company in best results. I attribute much of their success to Hamer's leadership."
- After 1995, I went back to the radio industry as a sales manager and had considerable success. Joel Oxley, a vice president with Hubbard Broadcasting, said, "While the market has struggled, Mike has led the news station in the right direction. Since he has been the general sales manager, WTOP has exceeded 28 out of 29 budgets."

Questions

1. What companies have you taken note of that outwardly express their efforts to be moral and righteous in selling and serving customers?

2. Do you hold any objections to the moral and ethical principles promoted in the Bible? Do you believe that being honest, loving, kind, and patient with people will always lead to satisfying results?

3. What serves as the final authority in your life? Is it the Bible, the Word of God? Or is it your conscience, reasoning ability, emotions, intellect, education, or personal experience?

Scriptural References

- The Bible should be the final authority for all decisions:

  All Scripture is God-breathed and is useful for teaching, rebuking, correcting and training in righteousness, so that the servant of God may be thoroughly equipped for every good work (2 Timothy 3:16–17).

- Biblical wisdom stays valuable forever:

  Heaven and earth will pass away, but my words will never pass away (Mark 13:31).

- The Word of God provides the most useful advice. It's living and active:

  For the word of God is living and active. Sharper than any double-edged sword, it penetrates even to dividing soul and spirit, joints and marrow; it judges the thoughts and attitudes of the heart (Hebrews 4:12).

- The ability to sell righteously comes through faith in Jesus Christ:

  This righteousness from God is given through faith in Jesus Christ to all who believe. There is no difference (Romans 3:22).

- Through the way He lived and died, Jesus made it possible for everyone to become righteous, which is the character or quality of being correct or just from a godly perspective:

  God made him who had no sin to be sin for us, so that in him we might become the righteousness of God (2 Corinthians 5:21).

- Jesus will supply all our needs and strengthen us to succeed righteously if we adhere to His teachings:

  I can do all this through him who gives me strength (Philippians 4:13).

- God can fulfill all our needs, even our needs while selling:

  And my God will meet all your needs according to the riches of his glory in Christ Jesus (Philippians 4:19).

CHAPTER 2:

Remain in Jesus

> "*Remain in me, as I also remain in you. No branch can bear fruit by itself; it must remain in the vine. Neither can you bear fruit unless you remain in me. I am the vine; you are the branches. If you remain in me and I in you, you will bear much fruit; apart from me you can do nothing.*"
>
> —John 15:4–5

Christ-Centered

More than two thousand years ago, shortly before His death and resurrection, Jesus gave His disciples instructions for leading fruitful lives. For our purposes, these instructions can direct us as we strive to sell righteously and successfully (fruitfully). Remaining in Jesus is the primary principle for selling God's way. This principle of remaining, remembering, and relying on the words and wisdom of Jesus arises out of the Gospel of John.

Jesus tells His disciples to remain in Him and that He will remain in them. Most people don't realize that we all have someone living in us, thus remaining in us, and we in them. These people occupy our thoughts, fuel our emotions, and direct our behavior. It might be a parent, teacher, enemy, friend, minister, manager, celebrity, coach, coworker, sibling, or spouse. These people might be believers or nonbelievers, but they can affect our lives in ways that can be fruitful or fruitless. Jesus instructs us to let the person living in us be Him. The Holy Spirit that Jesus Christ eloquently describes in the Gospel of John should be the inner person occupying our thoughts, fueling our emotions, and directing our behavior. As people selling righteously, this means that we make Jesus Lord over our selling lives. Jesus is our sales manager. His teachings and Spirit reside in and preside over all our sales and work-related activity.

To help us make decisions while selling, we can consider advice from others, defer to our own sense of reasoning, and reflect upon our experience. We can consult selling wisdom from books, seminars, and other resources, but the final authority as to what we must do should come from Christ-centered living.

Jesus Christ

Remaining in Jesus is the primary principle for selling God's way. Let His Holy Spirit be the person occupying your thoughts, fueling your emotions, and directing your behavior.

Fruit

Jesus says if we can remain in Him, allowing Him to remain in us, we will bear much fruit, and that apart from Him, we can do nothing. Biblical fruit can be good deeds or things that we do to help develop Christian disciples. But good fruit is also being led by God's Holy Spirit to be a living display of the nine attributes found in the following verses: "*But the fruit of the Spirit is love, joy, peace, forbearance* [patience], *kindness, goodness, faithfulness, gentleness and self-control. Against such things there is no law*" (Galatians 5:22–23).

Success God's Way

Many think the fruit of successful selling relates to money and position. However, confining the blessings of God to wealth and status is a mistake. In reading the stories of men like Abraham, Job, and David, we see they all gained great wealth and fame. But they also acquired things that allowed them to succeed during money problems and personal pain. God gave these people, and others like them, the fruit of the Spirit. If we sell God's way, we may earn large incomes and significant positions, but more importantly, the success we receive—the fruit we produce—includes love, joy, peace, patience, kindness, goodness, faithfulness, gentleness, and self-control.

> If we sell God's way, the success we receive can include large incomes and significant positions, but more importantly, it includes love, joy, peace, patience, kindness, goodness, faithfulness, gentleness, and self-control.

Love

The driving force behind our desire to sell righteously must be love, a love for God and a love for all people. One of the most important reasons to love God is because He loved us first. He demonstrated His great love for us by sending His only Son to die for our sins, offering each of us a new life that begins on earth through Christ and continues forever with God in Heaven. This love of God must motivate us to study the Bible so that we can correctly apply it to all aspects of living. In the Gospel of John, Jesus says two things about love that should compel us to sell God's way. He says that if we love Him, we'll obey His commandments, and He says that we should love one another as He has loved us (see John 13:34–35, John 14:15, and Romans 5:8).

Our love for others should drive us to interact with them in righteous ways. We should sell to others as if they were beloved family members. We need to interact with our prospects and customers in the same way we would want someone to interact with us if they loved us. Jesus says that people will know that we are His disciples if we love one another (see 1 Corinthians 13:4–10 and Romans 12:9–10).

Love

Our love for God should motivate us to study the Bible so that we can correctly apply it to all aspects of living. Our love for others should drive us to interact with them in righteous ways.

Joy

As believers, the joy we experience comes from the Holy Spirit that Jesus spoke about in the book of John. It's an internal sense of cheerful well-being that's not dependent on circumstances. This joy does not revolve around how much we sell or our relationship with other people. Our joy revolves around applying the teachings of Jesus to our lives at all times.

As people selling God's way, we are not exempt from the emotional and mental struggles that accompany selling. But when frustration and misfortune arrive to steal our joy, we can use the spiritual tools that God provides to reclaim (or maintain) our joy—tools such as prayer, fasting, and fellowship with other believers. The book of Psalms says the precepts of the Lord give joy to the heart and that weeping may endure for a night, but joy comes in the morning. As believers, we are instructed to always be joyful (see Psalm 19:8, Psalm 30:5, and 1 Thessalonians 5:16).

I've experienced times of unexplainable joy when the most natural thing for me to do would have been to sulk in sadness. Not only were sales slow, but the battle to make things better seemed to always end in defeat. Yet I still found myself in joyful anticipation of what would happen next, knowing that by applying Jesus's teachings, I'd either be made better by the battles or abundantly blessed with sales through the goodness of God's grace.

Peace

God offers a peace that surpasses all understanding. This peace empowers us to sell diligently without worry or fear, which can destroy a sale at any time. I've experienced fear of rejection and anxiety about approaching prospects, especially when I had no idea how welcoming a prospect would be. There were times I suspected a prospect was open to purchasing what I was selling but worry made me wonder if the timing was right to discuss what I was offering. By embracing the teachings of Jesus, I always found a peace that deflected any dread or discomfort, allowing me to go forward aggressively, regardless of what I was selling: eggs on the streets of Indiana, books to families in California, marketing programs to businesses in Washington, DC, or radio time to advertising agencies in New York City. Jesus tells us to seek righteousness and not to worry. He endows us with knowledge so that we can have peace (see Matthew 6:33–34, John 16:33, and Philippians 4:6–7).

Patience

The basic ingredients of any successful sales career include difficulties that could dislodge our confidence and replace it with discouragement. For example, most salespeople experience periods in their career of poor sales results when specific sales goals aren't met, and the fear of failing flings us further toward desperation and bad decisions. Also, forces outside the realm of sales results can negatively affect our attitude and effort.

My personal examples include divorce, a slumping economy, and a manager with a deceitful agenda. But despite what we encounter, I've learned that if we use the tools Christ provides, we'll find the patience needed to continue selling God's way, regardless of results or the amount of time it takes for our victories to arrive. There are several places in the Bible that provide instructions on how to be patient. The book of Hebrews advises us to fix our eyes on Jesus so that we do not grow weary and lose heart. Jesus tells us that if we ask anything in His name, He will do it for us. We just need to make sure whatever we ask for is something Jesus would want too (see John 14:13 and Hebrews 12:2–3).

I've worked in several places where the pressure to make a sale every day was intense, even though our buyers purchased on a weekly or monthly basis. Such selling environments breed impatience and improper sales techniques. I overcame these unrighteous forces in my work life by simply praying specifically against the intense pressure before and during each workday. In prayer, God always reminds me of three things:

- Be patient; God guarantees my victories in His promises.
- Labor as if I'm working for Him and not men.
- Be thankful I have a job, because my predicament could be much worse.

As part of my intimate, personal relationship with my loving God, I talk to Him, which is just one part of praying. The other part of prayer is *listening* to Him. Philippians 4:6 tells us not to worry about anything but to pray about everything: That means letting God speak into every circumstance, regardless of anxieties and any doubts we may hold. Many books and sermons are available to help us learn how to hear the voice of God. Rick Warren has a wonderful sermon entitled "Hearing the Voice of God" that you can find on the internet; Charles Stanley wrote a book entitled *How to Listen to God* that I think is fantastic.

Kindness

Through faith in Jesus Christ, we have received an abundance of kindness from God, even though each of us has succumbed to sin and our own evil desires; everyone's life gets marred by ungodly mistakes. We all deserve the wrath of God, along with being disqualified to receive His blessings. Yet God, in His loving-kindness, gives us the opportunity to be blessed greatly, even while selling, simply because we believe in Him, His Holy Spirit, and Jesus Christ as Lord and Savior.

Consequentially, as we remain in Jesus and rely on our faith is God, numerous opportunities to extend and receive kindness arise. As we extend kindness, the principle of reaping and sowing springs forth. As we plant kind seeds, others will show kindness toward us. If we approach problems with coworkers with a forgiving spirit and a "let's not blame anyone" attitude, then they will find it difficult to be unforgiving and blameful with us. If we interact with clients in a service-centered manner and solution-based effort, then clients will find it difficult to reject our service or find fault with our solutions. Naturally, under our own human power, it's impossible to be kind to everyone all the time. Remember that Jesus says we should love everyone, even our enemies. Only by surrendering to God's will can we find the wisdom to remain kind, regardless of circumstances or the unrighteous behavior of others (see 2 Corinthians 9:6, Ephesians 4:32, and 2 Timothy 1:7).

On several occasions, the sellers I managed or clients under my care made mistakes that lost revenue and damaged relationships. Such mistakes often aroused my anger along with a desire to accuse and assign blame. However, as a person following Jesus, I needed to extend kindness in the form of grace and forgiveness. To extend this type of kindness while working through mistakes and my own anger, I would pray. I'd ask God to give me the righteous words to say and the strength to be loving, kind, and patient, especially during confrontations.

Goodness

One of the Bible's most popular verses says that God works all things for the good of those who love Him, who have been called according to His purpose. This promise should motivate us to grow in our understanding of how to love Him. It should also motivate us to grasp a complete understanding of God's purpose for our lives. Through loving God and understanding His purpose for us, we can work confidently in any profession, knowing that regardless of what happens, we'll receive the goodness of the Lord.

The goodness we receive as salespeople can include money and status, along with far more valuable blessings, including satisfied customers who are strong advocates of what we sell and the way we sell it. Righteous relationships, optimal wisdom, and heavenly rewards are just a few of the good things we can receive through Christ-centered selling. The Bible overflows with biographies of believers whose righteousness and wisdom greatly exceeded their wealth; think of people like Boaz, Joseph, and Jabez. The book of Psalms says that those who seek the Lord lack no good thing. The greatest good we receive, as people who are selling God's way, is Jesus as sales manager. This means that if we let ourselves be managed by Jesus Christ, then we'll always be led to the best goodness. All our bad or sad days, career setbacks, income obstacles, and business relationships will be turned into good things (see Psalm 34:10 and Romans 8:28).

Faithfulness

As salespeople of faith, the greatest power we possess is our personal relationship with God. To access this power, we need to exercise our faith and trust God to lead us to the right things to say or do in all selling situations. The primary ways God directs us are through prayer, His Word, and Christian fellowship. God can supply us with the wisdom and energy needed to make sales or move us into a different career, if that is His will. Our faith in God must move us forward, even when it seems like following His wisdom will not lead to success.

My faith empowers me to take righteous actions, to make Christ-centered plans, and to envision earthly success. My faith also drops me to my knees in prayer and prompts me to study the Bible, humbly seeking wisdom. I believe that through God's love, I'll find the path that leads to victory, even when my circumstances have led me into darkness and despair. God promises that if we trust Him, He'll make our paths straight. If we lack wisdom, the Bible tells us that we should ask God for it and not doubt that He will give it to us. The Bible also says that godly wisdom is pure; peace-loving, considerate, submissive, and full of mercy and good fruit, while also being impartial and sincere (see Proverbs 3:5–6, James 1:5–8, and James 3:17).

Gentleness

Gentleness involves being compassionate and patient. Contrarily, I've witnessed companies that frequently encourage salespeople to rush prospects into buying decisions with no consideration given to the prospect's buying process. At that point, closing a sale and earning a commission become the driving passions, leading some salespeople to make false promises or malign the competition. But this type of behavior is not compassionate; this approach should never be used by anyone striving to be gentle.

The reputation salespeople have for being dishonest is well-earned. I've witnessed far too many managers inadvertently creating environments that encourage salespeople to fib, gossip, and slander. I've observed salespeople falsifying projections, faking sales, and forsaking righteous principles because of an unrighteous spirit that emanates from their manager, or some misguided internal motivation. Salespeople also behave sinfully because of an internal pressure that creates a fear of failure, which often morphs into a desperation that drives a salesperson to justify doing almost anything to make a sale and succeed or avoid losing their job. Any selling behavior born out of fear, greed, or self-serving ambitions is the antithesis of gentleness.

If we study the teachings of Jesus, we will see that embracing self-serving ambitions can lead to sinful behavior that can sabotage our sales and business relationships. When Christians sell in these ungentle ways, our convictions should kick in, causing shameful feelings to arise, because in our souls, we know that these things go against the teaching of Jesus. As people selling God's way, we don't need greed, guilt, or shame influencing our sales behavior. We must let Jesus remain in us so that gentleness gets incorporated into everything we do. We exhibit gentleness when we wait patiently for a prospect's answer, handle objections compassionately, or communicate clearly and honestly with a supervisor (see Philippians 2:3 and Ephesians 4:31).

I have had sales managers ask me to pester a prospect into buying to reach a sales goal. The problem with these requests was that they ignored the prospect's buying process and disregarded any previous arrangement the prospect and I had as to how the sale would be completed. Furthermore, such pushiness was rude, lacking tact and integrity. That way of selling often ignited uncomfortable feelings, because I needed to respectfully deny my manager's request or politely confront my prospect with terms and conditions not previously discussed. Some managers insisted on adding terms and conditions, such as these: "If you buy now, the company will lower the price and add extra benefits, but if you don't buy now, the company will raise the price and subtract something previously included." This type of selling lacks gentleness and is often done in guilt; it is motivated by greed or fear and needs to be discarded if we want to follow the teachings of Jesus, which says that we should always love and serve others.

Self-Control

The power to exercise self-control comes from God. The Lord provides all believers with the necessary tools for practicing self-control, which include faith, fasting, fellowship, giving, serving, prayer, praise, worship, and His Word (the Bible). Using these tools allows the Holy Spirit to guide us. Whenever we exhibit self-control, it shows that we are willingly allowing the Holy Spirit to direct our thoughts, feelings, and behavior. Our self-control demonstrates that we can allow biblical principles and ideologies to lead and comfort us, because we undoubtedly believe that there are no better principles and ideologies than the ones found in the Bible.

Before I became a committed Christian and began selling God's way, I concluded that some prospects and customers did not deserve my best sales effort and attitude. I came to this conclusion based upon a prospect's perceived revenue potential or some aspect of their personality that I found distasteful. But after I fully accepted Jesus Christ as both Lord and Savior, I received the Holy Spirit. This wonderful gift from God guided me to view everyone as someone to be loved and deserving of my best effort and attitude, regardless of circumstances or perceived personality clashes. Today, the Holy Spirit enables me to take control of my destructive thoughts and negative emotions. God's spirit of righteousness equips me to fight through every situation using tools like prayer and praise. I'm able to extend love to every prospect and client; I have a servant's attitude and make exhaustive efforts to meet their needs.

We need to closely examine our sales attitude and behavior to ensure we are exhibiting self-control. Every sinful act of disobedience and every thought that goes against the teaching of Jesus must be recognized, repented of, and released. Christian salespeople should be disciplining themselves to sell strictly according to biblical principles. Selling with this type of discipline demonstrates self-control and a love for doing things God's way (see Acts 1:8 and 1 Thessalonians 1:4–5).

Spiritual Selling Tools

The spiritual tools we sell with are faith, fasting, fellowship, giving, serving, prayer, praise, worship, and God's Word (the Bible). Using these tools allows the Holy Spirit to guide and comfort us.

Why Christ-Centered Selling?

Jesus Christ lived more than two thousand years ago in what is now known as the Middle East. Yet what He did and said impacts the lives of people today, all over the world. Millions of people have placed their faith in Him, and many have died because of their faith in Jesus. It may be hard for some to believe that through a staff of twelve men and numerous loyal women, the words and teachings of Jesus continue through generations, long after the death of His immediate followers.

Even if you are not a believer in Jesus Christ as Lord and Savior, you should want to know the convictions, principles, and words that made Him so persuasive and powerful. Surely, we all know it's wise to learn from the best. Throughout all of history, no other person has been as successful in changing lives and destinies as Jesus Christ. This is what makes doing anything God's way amazingly attractive and compelling. Furthermore, the Bible tells us that Jesus Christ is head over every power and authority. He can change circumstances, make things better, and he can change us as individuals. Leading us into a righteously productive life, which includes our sales life, where we repent from sins and cast all our cares on Him (see Colossians 2:8–10, Matthew 11:28, and Luke 5:32).

Questions

1. How often do you ask God in prayer for sales guidance and success?

2. What role does Jesus occupy in your work life? Why?

3. How do you define *success* in sales? Is loving and serving others part of that definition?

4. In what ways do you demonstrate love for your clients and coworkers?

Scriptural References

- What Jesus instructs us to do is to let the person living in us, occupying our thoughts, fueling our emotions, and directing our behavior be Him:

  "*Remain in me, as I also remain in you. No branch can bear fruit by itself; it must remain in the vine. Neither can you bear fruit unless you remain in me. I am the vine; you are the branches. If you remain in me and I in you, you will bear much fruit; apart from me you can do nothing*" (John 15:4–5).

- If we sell God's way, the success we receive can include money and position, but more importantly, it includes spiritual fruit:

  But the fruit of the Spirit is love, joy, peace, forbearance [patience], *kindness, goodness, faithfulness, gentleness and self-control. Against such things there is no law* (Galatians 5:22–23).

- Jesus says that we should love one another as He has loved us:

  "A new command I give you: Love one another. As I have loved you, so you must love one another. By this everyone will know that you are my disciples, if you love one another" (John 13:34–35).

- Jesus says that if we love Him, we'll obey His commandments:

  "If you love me, keep my commands" (John 14:15).

- God demonstrated His great love for us when He sent His only Son to die for our sins:

  But God demonstrates his own love for us in this: While we were still sinners, Christ died for us (Romans 5:8).

- Love is the motivating spirit for selling God's way:

  Love is patient, love is kind. It does not envy, it does not boast, it is not proud. It does not dishonor others, it is not self-seeking, it is not easily angered, it keeps no record of wrongs. Love does not delight in evil but rejoices with the truth. It always protects, always trusts, always hopes, always perseveres. Love never fails. But where there are prophecies, they will cease; where there are tongues, they will be stilled; where there is knowledge, it will pass away (1 Corinthians13:4–8).

Love must be sincere. Hate what is evil; cling to what is good. Be devoted to one another in love. Honor one another above yourselves (Romans 12:9–10).

- Jesus tells us to seek righteousness and not to worry:

But seek first his kingdom and his righteousness, and all these things will be given to you as well. Therefore do not worry about tomorrow, for tomorrow will worry about itself. Each day has enough trouble of its own (Matthew 6:33–34).

- Peace is found by embracing the teaching of Jesus:

"*I have told you these things, so that in me you may have peace. In this world you will have trouble. But take heart! I have overcome the world*" (John 16:33).

- God can give us a peace that surpasses all understanding:

Do not be anxious about anything, but in every situation, by prayer and petition, with thanksgiving, present your requests to God. And the peace of God, which transcends all understanding, will guard your hearts and your minds in Christ Jesus (Philippians 4:6–7).

- The Lord's precepts give joy to the heart:

The precepts of the Lord are right, giving joy to the heart. The commands of the Lord are radiant, giving light to the eyes (Psalm 19:8).

- For believers, there is always a way to reclaim our joy:

  For his anger lasts only a moment, but his favor lasts a lifetime; weeping may stay for the night, but rejoicing comes in the morning (Psalm 30:5).

- We're instructed to always be joyful:

  Rejoice always (1 Thessalonians 5:16).

  Jesus tells us that if we ask anything in His name, He will do it for us. We just need to make sure that whatever we ask for is something that Jesus would want too:

  "And I will do whatever you ask in my name, so that the Father may be glorified in the Son" (John 14:13).

- Focusing on Jesus helps us to be patient as we endure difficulties:

  Fixing our eyes on Jesus, the pioneer and perfecter of faith. For the joy set before him, he endured the cross, scorning its shame, and sat down at the right hand of the throne of God. Consider him who endured such opposition from sinners, so that you will not grow weary and lose heart (Hebrews 12:2–3).

- Extending kindness activates the principle of reaping and sowing, even while selling:

  Remember this: Whoever sows sparingly will also reap sparingly, and whoever sows generously will also reap generously (2 Corinthians 9:6).

- We need to be kind to coworkers and clients:

  Be kind and compassionate to one another, forgiving each other, just as in Christ God forgave you (Ephesians 4:32).

- The power to be kind and loving, regardless of circumstances, comes from God:

  For the Spirit God gave us does not make us timid, but gives us power, love and self-discipline (2 Timothy 1:7).

- As we seek to sell God's way, we will not lack anything that is good. Perhaps the greatest good we receive while selling this way is Jesus as sales manager:

  The lions may grow weak and hungry, but those who seek the Lord lack no good thing (Psalm 34:10).

- God works everything into goodness, for those who love Him:

  And we know that in all things God works for the good of those who love him, who have been called according to his purpose (Romans 8:28).

- In all selling situations, trusting God will lead us to do and say the right thing:

  Trust in the Lord with all your heart and lean not on your own understanding; in all your ways submit to him, and he will make your paths straight (Proverbs 3:5–6).

- Selling God's way gives us wisdom:

  If any of you lacks wisdom, you should ask God, who gives generously to all without finding fault, and it will be given to you. But when you ask, you must believe and not doubt, because the one who doubts is like a wave of the sea, blown and tossed by the wind. That person should not expect to receive anything from the Lord; such a person is double-minded and unstable in all they do (James 1:5–8).

- Godly wisdom comes with characteristics that confirm it's from heaven:

  But the wisdom that comes from heaven is first of all pure; then peace-loving, considerate, submissive, full of mercy and good fruit, impartial and sincere (James 3:17).

- Selling motivated by selfish ambitions or vain expectations is not selling righteously:

  Do nothing out of selfish ambition or vain conceit, but in humility consider value others above yourselves (Philippians 2:3).

- We must rid ourselves of slander and anger while selling:

  Get rid of all bitterness, rage and anger, brawling and slander, along with every form of malice (Ephesians 4:31).

- The Holy Spirit empowers us:

  But you will receive power when the Holy Spirit comes on you; and you will be my witnesses in Jerusalem, and in all Judea and Samaria, and to the ends of the earth (Acts 1:8).

- The Holy Spirit convicts us:

  For we know, brothers and sisters loved by God, that he has chosen you, because our gospel came to you not simply with words, but also with power, with the Holy Spirit and with deep conviction. You know how we lived among you for your sake (1 Thessalonians 1:4–5).

- Jesus Christ rules over every power and authority, follow His principles and precepts above all others:

  See to it that no one takes you captive through hollow and deceptive philosophy, which depends on human tradition and the elemental spiritual forces of this world rather than on Christ. For in Christ all the fullness of the Deity lives in bodily form, and in Christ you have been brought to fullness. He is the head over every power and authority (Colossians 2:8–10).

- Enter a personal relationship with Jesus Christ. There you will find rest from all your burdens and whatever makes you weary:

  "*Come to me, all you who are weary and burdened, and I will give you rest*" (Matthew 11:28).

- Jesus will help you sell righteously and forgive your past selling sins:

  "*I have not come to call the righteous, but sinners to repentance*" (Luke 5:32).

CHAPTER 3:

The Sales Process

The boys grew up, and Esau became a skillful hunter, a man of the open country, while Jacob was a quiet man, staying among the tents. Isaac, who had a taste for wild game, loved Esau, but Rebekah loved Jacob. Once when Jacob was cooking some stew, Esau came in from the open country, famished. He said to Jacob, "Quick, let me have some of that red stew! I'm famished!" (That is why he was also called Edom.) Jacob replied, "First sell me your birthright." "Look, I am about to die," Esau said. "What good is the birthright to me?" But Jacob said, "Swear to me first." So he swore an oath to him, selling his birthright to Jacob. Then Jacob gave Esau some bread and some lentil stew. He ate and drank, and then got up and left. So Esau despised his birthright.

—Genesis 25:27–34

Skillful Hunters

Esau selling his birthright to his twin brother Jacob represents the Bible's first sales transaction. The same God-given gifts that Esau used for hunting; he also used to sell his birthright (the product) to Jacob (the customer). The steps they went through to exchange stew for birthright give us a process for selling successfully today.

My Story

I am a career salesperson, having sold everything from eggs to advertising. I first used this process at age seven, selling eggs on the streets of Gary, Indiana, with my grandfather, a deeply religious man. He showed me this process and demonstrated how repeatable and reliable was. My grandfather paid me at the end of each sales day and treated me to dinner, so at a young age, I associated this process with earning revenue and rewards. My grandfather's best customers were loyal and bought eggs weekly. I noticed that his buyers acted more like friends than customers. He also found new customers in new places. These new customers reminded me of the old customers and their old places. My grandfather offered a warm greeting to everyone, even though he was very selective about who he chose to pursue as a customer. In getting people to buy, he never seemed pushy. He would always ask a lot of questions and present what seemed like the whitest, brightest, most perfectly shaped eggs. People seemed compelled to smile and simply say yes or no to buying the eggs. Some selling days ended poorly, but regardless of the outcome, my grandfather kept a pleasant disposition. The egg-selling era with my grandfather remains the most valuable period of my work life, because as we made sales calls, my grandfather emphasized three things: the inerrancy of the Bible, the power of prayer, and the importance of faith. At the time, I knew he was giving me instructions for living, but I realized later that those instructions also contained the concepts for selling successfully.

Almost a dozen years after my grandfather showed me this process, the Southwestern Company trained me in the same way. The Southwestern Company contracted me to sell books door-to-door in Los Angeles after my freshmen year of college at Boston University. The company frequently started training sessions by stating that in sales, if you put God first, the people around you second, and yourself third, you'll always come out on top. The first week selling door-to-door, I made twenty-five dollars. During my final month of selling books door-to-door, I made $400 a week. During my senior year of college, I landed a job selling advertising inside the playbill of a theater in Cambridge, Massachusetts. The theater manager was amazed by the number of ads that I sold using this process.

My first professional sales job after graduating from college required me to sell advertising for a small AM radio station in Falls Church, Virginia (a suburb of Washington, DC). The radio station didn't offer sales training. I started with a desk, a phone, and an opportunity to sell in the country's eighth-largest market. Very aware of the importance of succeeding at my first career opportunity, I relied on this process to sell a below-average product in an above-average competitive marketplace. I succeeded, eventually gaining the admiration of clients and coworkers. After almost two years of selling advertising at this small station, I secured a sales job at one of the leading FM radio stations in Washington, DC.

The process worked successfully in selling eggs for 35 cents in 1965 and for selling advertising for $350,000 in 2010. This process works in simple and complex sales, regardless of the number of decision-makers or factors that influence a buying decision. The process works regardless of the time it takes to complete a sale; it works in one day, and it works in one year.

The selling process that my grandfather showed me in the 1960s is the same process I use to sell successfully today. I am back to selling books (*Selling God's Way*); this time not door-to-door but heart-to-heart. Thankfully, because of God's grace, most of my workdays have ended celebrating sales victories, not dealing with defeats. Here is a question for you to ponder: If you deemphasized goal achievement and focused on refining and improving all aspects of your sales process, would you still achieve your goals? I believe that you would exceed your goals by strictly focusing on the process and refining it to achieve excellence in righteousness in every step.

Works Great!

I followed this process when I sold eggs for thirty-five cents and when I sold advertising for $350,000.

Today, many companies use this same process but assign different names and labels to each step. *Prospecting* may be viewed as *business development* and still include qualifying the prospects for sales success and revenue potential. I will cover the details for qualifying prospects in the chapter entitled "Prospecting." *Questioning* could be called *consulting* or *needs analysis* and involve several of the same strategies that I'll discuss later in this book. Many companies teach a sales process that involves more than seven steps. However, I have condensed this process into seven steps because in the Bible, the number seven is associated with completion. I've trained many successful salespeople using the seven-step process outlined in this chapter.

Seven-Step Sales Process

1. Committed and Competent
2. Prospecting
3. Questions
4. Presentations
5. Closing
6. Objections
7. Service

Committed and Competent

> *The boys grew up, and Esau became a skillful hunter, a man of the open country, while Jacob was a quiet man, staying among the tents.*
>
> —Genesis 25:27

Just as Esau became a skillful hunter, we need to become skillful sellers. Each of us needs to continually be involved in sales training, either formally or informally. I'm constantly reading the Bible and other books, and I also get advice from other sales executives to grow in my ability to sell successfully. We should all be students of life and sales. Studying, analyzing, and applying what we learn makes life better for ourselves and people everywhere.

While we are born with certain talents and personality traits that directly lend themselves to successful selling, none of us is born with business, customer, or product knowledge. So, we must make a commitment and take action to acquire specific business and industry knowledge, especially as it pertains to the products and customers that we and our competitors sell.

Our people skills should continually be a work in progress, evident by an ongoing improvement in our relationships with customers and coworkers, the people that we want to sell to or serve with excellence. Our commitment provides the fuel that drives our competency to a level of excellence. Operating with excellence and selling righteously, we'll experience fewer disruptions in our sales process, because we won't repeatedly make the same mistakes. Chapter 4 discusses in detail what commitment and competency look like as it relates to selling.

Prospecting

> *Once when Jacob was cooking some stew, Esau came in from the open country, famished.*
>
> —Genesis 25:29

Prospecting involves identifying people and orchestrating meetings with anyone who can say yes or no to buying what we sell. Prospecting entails being prepared to begin a sales process whenever someone approaches us or whenever we approach a potential prospect. Esau found Jacob who could say yes or no to exchanging food for his birthright. As people selling God's way, we should hunger for sales and search righteously for ways to satisfy that need. Esau, being famished, identified Jacob as a person who could potentially provide what he needed. He approached Jacob and began the sales process.

Chapter 5 digs into prospecting and reveals how the principles Jesus used more than two thousand years ago to take people through a process of spiritual growth are still applicable today for taking people through a sales process.

Be Prepared

Prospecting entails being prepared whenever someone approaches us or whenever we approach a potential prospect.

Questioning

> *He said to Jacob, "Quick, let me have some of that red stew! I'm famished!" (That is why he was also called Edom.) Jacob replied, "First sell me your birthright."*
>
> —Genesis 25:30–31

During the questioning stage, we analyze the situation, work on the relationship, and discover what needs to be presented. Chapter 6 covers the questioning stage of the sales process, arguably the most important because righteous relationships are constructed during questioning. Esau's demanding question reflected his obstinate position and set the tone for a relationship that later would become disruptive.

One of the major goals of questioning is to gather enough of the right type of information so we'll know what to present. During this time, we also get a better understanding of the customer's buying process. Of course, we need the prospect's cooperation during this stage, answering questions, and in some selling scenarios, giving the assignment of what needs to be presented. Prospects cooperate if they think we can solve a problem or maximize an opportunity. The opportunity to receive the wealth and status associated with Esau's birthright motivated Jacob to cooperate during this stage. In his reply to Esau's question, Jacob gave him the assignment of presenting that birthright.

Presenting

> *"Look, I am about to die," Esau said. "What good is the birthright to me?"*
>
> —Genesis 25:32

Chapter 7 contains instructions for delivering presentations. In that stage, we see solutions and opportunities wrapped in benefits. These benefits are presented by the salesperson, wrapped inside a vision of the future. Where the customer receives what we sell, and all parties are righteously satisfied.

The information gathered in the previous stages impacts the quality of the presentation. During the questioning stage, Jacob revealed that the birthright was needed. Esau presented him the birthright in the context of a future in which he saw himself dead and the birthright useless. Esau devalued his own product; even though the birthright came with great benefits, which was why he later regretted selling it. As the son now entitled to the birthright, Jacob would receive a double portion of their father's inheritance, along with the leadership position in the family (see Hebrews 12:16–17).

Also, during this stage, the focus shifts from the prospect's needs to what we sell. The prospect's level of attentiveness should rise because they sense a viable solution or worthwhile opportunity forthcoming. Unfortunately, a salesperson's self-serving ambitions can hijack a sales presentation, leading a seller to do or say things that can devalue or inflate the benefits of what's being presented. This can be seen when salespeople exaggerate benefits or lower prices to complete a sale, sometimes to their own detriment. During the above presentation, Esau, being famished, valued food more than the birthright, making his highly esteemed birthright something he sold for mere stew.

Closing

So he swore an oath to him, selling his birthright to Jacob.

—Genesis 25:33

Closing is the essence of a salesperson's job. It's diligently doing the right things to complete a sale. It typically involves an action we must initiate to get a contract, agreement, or payment. Although there are several ways to successfully close a sale, depending on what we sell, our closing behavior should always include a principle, program, and promise. The truth, the facts and benefits regarding our product build the closing principle. This principle should motivate the prospect to help us complete the sale. The help the prospect provides is tangible action steps. These actions steps dictate the program. And the promise predicts the future if the prospect accepts the principle, and the program is enacted, by either the salesperson or prospect. Chapter 8 covers closing.

In Esau and Jacob's sales transaction, the closing principle is the highly esteemed birthright, which guaranteed its owner exclusive benefits. The swearing of an oath represented the closing program. These were the action steps needed for Esau to complete to close the sale, the selling of his birthright to Jacob, his brother. And the closing promise is the vision of a future, where Jacob sees himself owning a double portion of their father's inheritance, along with the leadership position in the family, after the sale is completed.

Objections

> *But Jacob said, "Swear to me first."*
>
> —Genesis 25:33

In this scenario, the above Scripture comes before the previous one associated with closing a sale. However, most objections come after your close is attempted. Please remember that objections can arise at any time, even in the prospecting stage. An objection reveals a position held by the prospect that is an obstacle to completing the sale. Chapter 9 explores objections. An objection arises from the prospect's perspective; for example, they may say your price is too high or request changes to the final contract. Objections help us develop our powers to persuade and persevere, enabling us to acquire every skill needed for building a successful sales career.

Jacob's distrust of Esau created an obstacle that surfaced as an objection. As part of their closing program, Jacob wanted Esau to swear over the birthright before he handed over the stew. This would defuse his trust issue and destroy the possibility that this objection might end Esau's sales process. It's not stated how or when Esau acquired oath-swearing skills, but he used those skills to complete the sale. Esau swore the oath, dissolved the objection, and then closed the sale, exchanging his birthright for stew, so that he would no longer be in his perceived unbearable hunger.

Objections Help

Objections assist us in developing our powers to persuade and persevere and help us to acquire every skill needed for building a successful sales career.

Servicing

Then Jacob gave Esau some bread and some lentil stew. He ate and drank, and then got up and left. So Esau despised his birthright.

—Genesis 25:34

During this stage, people selling God's way deliver what we sold and demonstrate gratitude for the sale. Service involves meeting the needs of others. At times, it requires us to listen attentively, so that we can follow instructions explicitly. At other times, it calls for observation, so that we can anticipate needs. Excellence in serving calls for a righteous attitude along with a well-constructed plan to deliver superior service. Chapter 10 discusses the seven ways to deliver superior service.

In the sales transaction found in the book of Genesis, Esau immediately eats the stew to satisfy his self-serving desires, and Jacob eventually takes delivery of the birthright. With that transaction Jacob owns the leadership position in his family, which came with the birthright; later God changes his name to Israel and makes him the patriarch of a nation that still survives today. Thankfully, through God's grace and guidance, the birthright sold for stew, effectively served not only Jacob and Esau, but billions of people throughout hundreds of generations.

Journeying through the Process

The journey through the sales process always starts with being committed and competent. How we transition from one stage to another depends on who we sell to, what we sell, and the day we expect to close the sale because customers use different buying processes. For example, prospects often approach salespeople with questions about pricing, which leads to presentations. In those instances, after the presentation, it is best for people selling righteously to return to the prospecting stage to qualify the prospect, in hopes of finding someone who has the potential to become an ideal satisfied customer.

At times, prospects have more than one decision-maker, with each decision-maker asserting different forms of influence. As a result, the salesperson may be in different stages of the sales process at the same time, because the potential customer consists of different people at different stages in their buying process. This also means the day we anticipate closing the sale depends upon when we think the most influential decision-makers will need our product or solution.

The more sophisticated buyers, like those I encountered selling advertising in New York City, dictated when to transition from one stage to another. With New York buyers, I would always take the first step by being committed and competent, but the buyer's purchasing process dictated my next step. At times, I would skip from being committed and competent straight to the objection stage. My move to this stage often came if I hadn't received a request for a proposal at this point in the process. At other times, I would go from being committed and competent to the questioning stage, just to uncover the prospect's buying process.

Transitioning through the stages involves merging our sales process with the prospect's buying process. We always start by being committed and competent, but where we go after that and how we sequence through the stages depends on who we are selling to and the steps in their buying process.

Time in the Process

How much time we spend in each stage of the sales process depends on what we sell and the prospect's ability to understand what we are offering. As a youth selling eggs, the entire sales process could take anywhere from five to fifteen minutes because the customers' understanding of eggs and how they work was relatively complete. Also, our rival egg sellers weren't aggressive or predatory. I would spend most of my time in the closing and servicing stages, helping a customer make the decision to buy and providing the eggs at the proper time.

In selling advertising, the sales process could take as long as a year because the prospect would need convincing that radio advertising worked and education on how my radio station could help. Also, I encountered competition from other media and radio stations, and at times, the competition was aggressive.

The quantity and quality of competition play an important role in getting people to buy. The more choices they have, the more time prospects may take to decide. Quality competition means that the salesperson needs to spend more time prospecting because the pool of potential buyers fluctuates.

At times, while selling advertising, the sales process could be completed over one or two days because the buyers were sophisticated professionals. They would contact radio stations with their buying processes completely prepared. Examples are companies like Coke, McDonald's, or Toyota: Their ad agencies understood how radio advertising worked, and they were prepared to buy and quickly implement their marketing campaign. Customers like these wanted me to sell quickly, enabling them to move to other priorities. However, other prospects could require a yearlong sales process, especially if I approached them selling a marketing campaign that was outside their normal advertising activity.

If the sales process provides a complete understanding of the product and how it works, then the process usually lasts a relatively short amount of time, often less than a day. A short sales process was typical when I sold books door-to-door. In these scenarios, most of the selling time is spent closing and servicing. However, if what we sell requires education, then the sales process is longer, perhaps as long as a year, especially if competition exists. A longer sales process requires us to spend more time in the prospecting stage, finding and qualifying customers, and in the presentation stage, explaining what we sell, so that the prospect has a satisfactory understanding of the benefits being offered.

Completing Sales Processes

How much time we spend in each stage of a sales process depends on what is being sold and the prospect's comprehension of what is being offered. How we transition through the stages depends on who we are selling to and the steps in their buying process. Of course, the Word of God shapes what we do in each stage.

Questions

1. What is your sales process?

2. Do you spend a lot of time in any stages of your sales process? Why those stages? Does this need to change?

3. What are your customers' buying processes? What stages do they go through physically, mentally, and emotionally as they decide whether to buy your product or service?

4. If you downplayed the importance of sales goals and focused on refining your sales process, building up each stage in the areas of excellence and righteousness, would you still achieve your goals?

Scriptural References

- The Bible's first sales transaction is one brother selling his birthright to his twin brother:

  Jacob replied, "First sell me your birthright" (Genesis 25:31).

- A salesperson's self-serving desire to make a sale can highjack a sales process, leading them to do or say things that misrepresent the benefits of what's being sold (at times, even to their own detriment). Esau presented his birthright to Jacob as something that would eventually be useless. He devalued his own product, a selling error he later regretted:

  See that no one is sexually immoral, or is godless like Esau, who for a single meal sold his inheritance rights as the oldest son. Afterward, as you know, when he wanted to inherit this blessing, he was rejected. Even though he sought the blessing with tears, he could not change what he had done (Hebrews 12:16–17).

- Even though a person may be born with talents and a personality suited for professional selling, all salespeople must learn business processes and hone their skills to become committed and competent sellers:

  The boys grew up, and Esau became a skillful hunter, a man of the open country, while Jacob was a quiet man, staying among the tents (Genesis 25:27).

- One of the first steps in prospecting involves finding someone who is hungry for what we sell, much like Jacob, who came across the hungry Esau:

  Once when Jacob was cooking some stew, Esau came in from the open country, famished (Genesis 25:29).

- As righteous salespeople, it's always best to question prospects before selling anything. That way, we can determine what we should sell and how we should sell it:

  He said to Jacob, "Quick, let me have some of that red stew! I'm famished!" (That is why he was also called Edom.) Jacob replied, "First sell me your birthright" (Genesis 25:30–31).

- During the presentation stage of the sales process, the prospect's level of attentiveness should rise because of the benefits being offered and their desire for those benefits. This is a strong signal that we can proceed with closing the sale:

  "Look, I am about to die," Esau said. "What good is the birthright to me" (Genesis 25:32)?

- In the closing stage, we must righteously complete all the necessary steps to get a contract, agreement, or payment:

  So he swore an oath to him, selling his birthright to Jacob (Genesis 25:33).

- During the sales process, objections that are obstacles to closing a sale may arise. At the same time, handling objections helps us perfect our selling skills:

  But Jacob said, "Swear to me first (Genesis 25:33)!

- In the service stage of the sales process, we deliver our product and oversee customer satisfaction:

  Then Jacob gave Esau some bread and some lentil stew. He ate and drank, and then got up and left. So Esau despised his birthright (Genesis 25:34).

CHAPTER 4:

Committed and Competent

Watch out for false prophets. They come to you in sheep's clothing, but inwardly they are ferocious wolves. By their fruit you will recognize them. Do people pick grapes from thorn bushes, or figs from thistles? Likewise, every good tree bears good fruit, but a bad tree bears bad fruit. A good tree cannot bear bad fruit, and a bad tree cannot bear good fruit. Every tree that does not bear good fruit is cut down and thrown into the fire. By their fruit you will recognize them.

—Matthew 7:15–20

Your Fruit

The first step in your sales process needs to be a commitment to becoming and remaining competent. Your level of competency reflects your level of commitment. The fruit you bear reflects your commitment to selling righteously and your competency as it relates to product and customer knowledge. Hopefully, we will be able to look back on our sales career and see an abundance of satisfied and successful customers, which is good fruit. Salespeople often fail to produce good fruit when they don't know all aspects of their own product or when they fail to comprehend and respond to a customer's needs.

Selling with poor product and customer knowledge prevents us from bearing good fruit, because this lack of knowledge will eventually embed dissatisfaction or indifference into the customer's mind, regarding what we sell, even building up a disdain for the process we use to sell it. For people selling righteously, customer dissatisfaction, disdain, and indifference is bad fruit. The last thing we need is for our income and business relationships to be damaged by a lack of knowledge that produced too much bad selling fruit (see Hosea 4:6).

We need to implement practices that keep us in a learning and growing mode as it pertains to product and customer knowledge; this keeps a lack of knowledge from hindering our production of good fruit. As I discussed in chapter 2, good fruit can include money and promotions, along with far more valuable blessings, such as a tremendous number of well-served, satisfied customers, who are strong advocates for what we sell and the way we sell it.

We must be prepared to learn and grow continually because things change. Emerging technologies, government regulations, and transformative data can cause market conditions to change not only what is being sold, but how it's packaged, presented, and delivered. Telephones, typewriters, and taxi cabs gave way to mobile phones, iPads, and Uber. Many items that used to be bought through face-to-face transactions with a salesperson can now be purchased online. The first step in continuous growth is a commitment to maintaining a level of excellence in product and customer knowledge. A righteous seller is like a skillful hunter who excels in tracking-prospecting, weaponry (product knowledge), and animal information (customer knowledge).

Level of Excellence

A hunter's level of excellence is manifested in the constant capture of game along with the capacity to consistently use what's caught to meet needs. Sometimes, it's the hunter's personal needs that are being satisfied, and at other times it's the needs of their family or community. Likewise, a salesperson's level of excellence is manifested in the consistent completion of sales and the continual establishment of righteous relationships that cultivate even more sales. This way, needs are continually being satisfied, be it the needs of that excellent salesperson, or their family, career, and community.

Excellent hunters and salespeople often reap rewards and recognition for their ability to consistently meet needs. For example, as we are reminded in Genesis 25:27–34, the Bible's first sales transaction, Isaac, Esau's father, had a taste for wild game and loved Esau. Thus, Esau was highly esteemed by his father, partially because of his ability to hunt well and consistently deliver wild game. Salespeople are often among the top income earners in a company because of their ability to consistently bring in the highly valued and much-needed revenue.

Product Knowledge

Committed and competent salespeople need a complete understanding of their product, just as skillful hunters need a complete understanding of their weapon. In selling, our product is our weapon; we use it for capturing customers just like hunters use their weapons for capturing animals. The prospects we approach, how we communicate, and our contribution to society all revolve around the product we sell.

Inaccurate product knowledge may lead the salesperson to approach the wrong prospects, communicate incorrect information, and provide poor customer service. This also prevents the seller from communicating all that could go wonderfully well with their product and all that could go awry with their service, opening the door to customer dissatisfaction. As a salesperson communicates flawed information regarding their product's possibilities and limitations, business opportunities and commissions are lost, and time is wasted all because of a seller working with insufficient or faulty product knowledge. The product, our weapon, can be used constructively if crafted and handled correctly by righteously motivated individuals. On the other hand, our product could cause destruction if it is handled incorrectly by someone regardless of their intentions.

As people selling God's way, we must invest time in learning all aspects of our product, from its origins to the future of the industry. We need to know how our product works from the first day it's purchased to the very last day it's used. We also need to know what needs to be done so that our product won't fail and how to fix things if something does go wrong. This allows honesty to flourish as we communicate features and benefits, along with possibilities and limitations. A cornerstone of doing anything God's way includes honesty. It pleases God and ushers in guidance and endurance (see Proverbs 11:3 and 21:6).

Customer Knowledge

A skillful hunter garners expert knowledge of the game being hunted, much in the same way we need to attain expert knowledge of the customers we seek. The service we provide and how we build a righteous relationship revolve around our customer knowledge. We need to know our customers' demographics, lifestyle, inclinations, and buying processes. In the early stages of becoming excellent in sales, we should learn about our customers in a very general sense, from a big-picture point of view. But as we progress and work with clients individually, we should acquire specific information as it pertains to their personalities, and priorities.

We'll eventually use that information to approach the best prospects and righteously sell what's needed at the time it's needed, transforming our customer knowledge into service-focused selling. If all goes well, our customers produce repeat contracts-sales, positive reviews, and referrals that will serve us and our company, by helping us to earn a substantial income and profits. Much like a skillful hunter who uses their knowledge of animals to select a target to hunt, in the best possible season for catching that specific animal. After capturing their target, they turn the animal into products that will serve as clothes and food for their family.

Customer knowledge will also prove valuable as we attempt to deliver superior service. If we desire greatness as salespeople, we must deliver great customer service. We should want our customers to have a great buying experience and become strong advocates for our products and services. In chapter 12, I'll examine how customer service relates to greatness. Jesus said that whoever wants to be great must be a servant, that whoever wants to be greatest must be a servant to all (see Mark 10:43–44).

My Customer and Product Knowledge Story

After seven years of selling radio advertising, I earned a promotion into sales management. I believe that it was due to my significant number of satisfied clients and consistent goal achievement. To become a successful sales manager, I needed to transfer all day-to-day duties of managing my accounts to other salespeople. Some of the more memorable compliments I received came from my previous clients telling my replacements that they didn't expect immediate results after their commercials aired. This surprised my replacements because clients typically expect an instant return from their advertising, most often in the form of inquiries and visits. Exactly what happens after a commercial airs remains almost impossible to predict. The most a salesperson should promise is that radio advertising will be delivered to a specific audience in a favorable format. A client's advertising investment could result in a phone call or in a potential customer just remembering they exist. Nevertheless, many radio salespeople, in the past and today, do a disservice by allowing clients to believe that their assessment of advertising expenditures should revolve around the number of inquiries after a commercial airs. This disservice increases the potential for customer dissatisfaction, which leads to terminated contracts and damaged relationships because of unfulfilled expectations.

Product and Customer Knowledge

Committed and competent salespeople need a complete understanding of their products and customers. The service we provide and the establishment of righteous relationships revolve around customer knowledge. The prospects we approach, how we communicate, and our contribution to society all revolve around product knowledge.

During my years selling radio advertising, I avoided these scenarios by explaining how my product, radio advertising, worked and how advertising generally worked. My formal education at Boston University included enough advertising and marketing courses to declare both disciplines as concentrations. My informal education included reading books, attending seminars, and networking with other successful salespeople. Through a God-directed desire to learn, I reached a level of excellence in product and customer knowledge that empowered me to communicate truth. I could clearly and honestly explain how my product worked while pointing out its limitations as to what a client could expect. The customer knowledge I acquired allowed me to interact effectively with prospects who wanted an instant return on their advertising investment. It also allowed me to strategize with my prospects on the best way for them to get customers, which was one of their top priorities.

My education and experience equipped me with the knowledge needed to capture customers and transform them into long-term clients who spoke highly of me to others. It also allowed me to communicate confidently that radio advertising did not always generate tangible direct results—in fact, most of the time, it did not. Additionally, I was able to explain how advertising worked in a client's overall quest to get customers. To me, it was important not to overpromise but to have clients align their expectations around my professional analysis of their situation, even if it required me to communicate unpleasant information. This allowed me to build righteous business relationships based on honesty. These types of relationships endured, even after my direct involvement with the client ended.

Seek God First

As people selling God's way, we must seek God's will first to confirm that our career path includes a sales job. It's important not to read this book and find a way to fit God into your career plans; instead, read the Bible and find your career path in God's plan. Pursuing a sales career that fits within God's will must provide the motivation for becoming committed and competent. God's desire, not our own, must be the driving force behind all we do as believers. God plans to give us a fantastic future if we seek Him with all our heart. If we commit our ways to God and find delight in the things of God, then He will give us the desires of our hearts (see Psalm 37:4–6 and Jeremiah 29:11).

Many reliable tools are available to help you determine whether God's will for our life includes selling professionally. The church I belong to offers a class on recognizing your spiritual gifts. The most powerful tools I've used give priority to prayer, Bible study, and serving others. In the book *Experiencing God*, the author Henry T. Blackaby, puts forth the concept that God is always at work around us, continually pursuing a loving relationship with each one of us that is real and personal. God is inviting each one of us to become involved with Him and engage in His work.

God's Will

It's important not to read *Selling God's Way* and find a way to fit God into your career plans; instead, read the Bible and find your career path in God's plan.

Easy Entry

I see far too many salespeople who belong in other professions. This is because entry into a sales career remains relatively easy, despite the significant number of companies that attempt to eliminate unqualified applicants by using tools like the Myers-Briggs and Gallup personality tests, tools that help determine a person's potential for sales success.

A job in sales should (but does not) require graduate-level coursework or a specialized degree, like those earned by doctors or lawyers. However, I hope the day arrives when a formal education in sales becomes mandatory for all sellers, with all salespeople required to pass a standardized test after completing specific courses. Hopefully, I'll see the day when colleges and universities offer courses that cover all aspects of professional selling, classes on business presentations, business development, prospecting, and customer service. The sales industry needs well-educated people who possess the appropriate natural talents and spiritual gifts.

Talents and Gifts

A person does not have to be scientific or artistic to succeed at selling, but they should possess certain natural talents and spiritual gifts. Everyone is born with certain talents, and everyone has access to the spiritual gifts that are available through accepting Jesus Christ as Lord and Savior.

The spiritual gifts needed to sell successfully and righteously are *knowledge*, *exhortation*, and *mercy*. Knowledge relates to a person's ability to discover and understand information. Exhortation allows a person to righteously comfort and encourage others. Mercy gives one the ability to sympathize and empathize with others, especially those with exorbitant needs.

The innate talents required for selling successfully are *persuasion*, *service*, and *communication*. Persuasive powers give a salesperson the ability to convince others to buy. Service instincts guide a salesperson to meet needs, which is key in generating referrals and repeat customers. Communication skills help a salesperson to speak, listen, and write effectively so that the information communicated arrives unaccompanied by confusion or carelessness.

Anyone possessing those spiritual gifts and natural talents can sell in a way that righteously maximizes their income as they build the best possible business relationships. However, anyone who consistently experiences an internal sense of discomfort while selling, along with a frustration in grasping the basic concepts of selling, should examine whether a sales career is appropriate for them.

Sales Skills

After we determine that sales is our God-directed career path, the next step is to make a commitment to that calling by developing an exemplary set of sales skills. Company training programs, how-to-sell books, seminars, networking, and the actual experience of selling all help in becoming an excellent salesperson. Of course, the most important thing is to have a personal relationship with Jesus Christ. This allows the Holy Spirit to counsel and comfort as a person soars or struggles in any profession.

Unbreakable Belief

A major step toward becoming an excellent salesperson involves selling something that arouses an unbreakable belief that the product or service works, that it righteously fulfills what it promises. This allows us to sell with grace and gratitude, not with greed and guilt. Unbreakable belief is communicated through eye contact, contract terminology, body language, spoken words, and consistent follow-through. This belief can arise out of several sources, such as the straightforward simplicity of what's being sold or evidence of substantial revenue and profits. Even our intellect and intuition can serve as catalysts to our belief that what we sell, or what we're about to sell, works and serves customers righteously. Appliances, airplanes, and autos are examples of products that salespeople can believe in because of their simplicity and history of significant revenue. Analyzing information such as a company's years in business, employee turnover, industry reputation, and stock prices can also lead a salesperson to accept or reject the belief that what they sell works. Our product should undoubtedly fulfill what is expected and serve as anticipated.

Righteousness and Belief

As people selling God's way, we must hold an unbreakable belief that our product or service works and that it righteously fulfills what it promises. This allows us to sell with grace and gratitude, not with greed and guilt.

If we need to use deceit and dishonesty in the process of selling anything, then we should commit to selling something else. If selling a product requires us to deviate from being truthful and transparent, it is not worth selling; furthermore, having to use deceit and dishonesty invalidates our belief in what we are trying to sell and how we sell it. Please note, if we're unable to consistently make sales and build righteous relationships by meeting customer needs, even though we're committed and competent sellers, then something is wrong with what we sell or how we sell it.

When committed, competent salespeople find themselves in a cycle of consistent disappointment, they need to assess whether the product they sell or the sales process is failing to live up to their initial expectations when they took the sales position. This situation may mean committing to selling something else or discarding the process used to sell that product. In other words, what they're trying to sell and how they're trying to sell it may not be meeting their needs or the customer's needs. When skillful hunters consistently return home without game and are unable to meet the needs of their family because they're using a defective bow or shoddy arrows, then a drastic change needs to occur with the weapons they use to hunt.

Something's Wrong

If we're unable to consistently close sales and establish righteous relationships by meeting customer needs even though we're committed and competent sellers, then something is wrong with what we sell or how we sell it.

Questions

1. How would you rate your product and customer knowledge on a scale of one to ten? Why did you give yourself that score?

2. Do you hold an expert's level of knowledge about your product, from its origins to projected future?

3. Do you have a process in place for continual learning as it relates to your industry and the product you sell? When was the last time someone asked you a question about your product and you didn't know the answer?

4. What are your natural talents and spiritual gifts, the characteristics endowed to you by God and nature? Do these abilities directly lend themselves to selling successfully and righteously?

Scriptural References

- The Bible says that people are destroyed by a lack of knowledge. The last thing any of us needs is sales careers and business relationships destroyed by our lack of product or customer knowledge:

  My people are destroyed from lack of knowledge. "Because you have rejected knowledge, I also reject you as my priests; because you have ignored the law of your God, I also will ignore your children" (Hosea 4:6).

- If we commit our ways to God and find delight in the things of God, then the Lord will give us the desires of our hearts:

  Take delight in the Lord, and he will give you the desires of your heart. Commit your way to the LORD; trust in him and he will do this: He will make your righteous reward shine like the dawn, your vindication like the noonday sun (Psalm 37:4–6).

- God plans to prosper us, to give us a hope and a future:

  "For I know the plans I have for you," declares the Lord, "plans to prosper you and not to harm you, plans to give you hope and a future" (Jeremiah 29:11).

- Our integrity will guide us as we sell righteously:

  The integrity of the upright guides them, but the unfaithful are destroyed by their duplicity (Proverbs 11:3).

  A fortune made by a lying tongue is a fleeting vapor and a deadly snare (Proverbs 21:6).

- Jesus talked about the relationship between greatness and serving:

  Not so with you. Instead, whoever wants to become great among you must be your servant, and whoever wants to be first must be slave of all (Mark 10:43–44).

CHAPTER 5:

Prospecting

I will show you what he is like who comes to me and hears my words and puts them into practice. He is like a man building a house, who dug down deep and laid the foundation on rock. When a flood came, the torrent struck that house but could not shake it, because it was well built. But the one who hears my words and does not put them into practice is like a man who built a house on the ground without a foundation. The moment the torrent struck that house, it collapsed and its destruction was complete.

—Luke 6:47–49

Foundation on Rock

Around the year AD 30, Jesus taught the Sermon on the Mount near the Sea of Galilee; more than five thousand people journeyed to hear Him explain how to live righteously. Using the parable of a wise and foolish builder, Jesus illustrated the importance of being a doer of the Word and not just a hearer. This illustration provides valuable insight into prospecting, because finding customers is like building a house. Both endeavors require a process that produces provisions. Houses provide shelter and comfort, and customers produce sales that provide income.

Just as a wise builder digs deep to lay a foundation on solid rock, a wise salesperson digs deep to find a prospect, the right type of potential customer, and sets that foundation or prospect on biblical rock (the Word of God). To sell righteously, we must prospect thoroughly to find the right type of customers and interact with them on the bases of biblical principles. This allows us to survive and thrive during difficulties, like the wise builder whose house survives during a storm because its foundation rests on immovable rock. Foolish salespeople and foolish builders do not dig deep enough or investigate prospects thoroughly enough to set their foundation on something that stays the same forever, like the Word of God, our immovable rock. During difficulties, they experience destruction (see 1 Peter 1:25).

Prospecting Righteously

A wise salesperson digs deep to find a prospect, the right type of potential customer, and sets their foundation or prospect on biblical rock (the Word of God).

Digging Deep: Three Goals

Digging deep is a process of discovery because we're trying to find a well-qualified prospect, who has the potential to become a great customer. This digging-deep process must be repeatable because we always need customers—either completely new customers or former customers returning to the sales process as prospects.

We have three goals while digging deep. The first goal is to develop a target prospect list. The second goal revolves around meetings. The third goal, often referred to as "qualifying," requires us to determine the prospect's potential to become a satisfied customer. In selling God's way, we also look for evidence of righteousness. Some customers can act like angels, while others can behave more like demons. Doing business with prospects who possess righteous values allows honesty and loyalty to flourish, as it builds a road to resolving conflicts with minimal discomfort. I have discovered through far too many painful experiences that doing business with unrighteous customers eventually leads to negative consequences. Jesus and Paul both spoke about being mindful of the people we associate with (see Matthew 7:6 and 1 Corinthians 15:33).

All three prospecting goals can be completed simultaneously. I can compile a list of targets, arrange meetings, and qualify prospects while looking for evidence of their righteousness during a meeting with just one potential prospect. What's important is to spend significant time prospecting, digging deep through information, and contacting people on the target prospect list. We also need to set a minimum number of appointments each week: these are meetings with people who can say yes to buying what we sell or influence whether our product gets bought or rejected. In selling advertising, I aspired to prospect—to dig deep—for a minimum of ten hours each week and arrange at least five appointments. If you're new in sales or starting a sales job at a new company, you should dedicate a minimum of 50 percent of your work hours to prospecting each week.

Shortly before ascending into heaven, Jesus gave His disciples the command to prospect for souls. This is often called the Great Commission. As people selling God's way, connecting with prospects constitutes our Great Commission, whether the prospect finds us, or we find the prospect (see Matthew 28:18–19).

Avoid Unscrupulous Prospects

Doing business with prospects who possess righteous values allows honesty and loyalty to flourish. It also opens a path to resolving conflicts with minimal discomfort. Jesus and Paul both spoke about being mindful of the people we associate with.

Goal One: The Prospect List

Digging deep starts by making a list of target prospects, like a wise builder who makes a list of the materials needed. Prospects should be people and companies. We start by identifying the characteristics of an angelic customer, since we need prospects with the same attributes. A review of our best customers helps us create a profile of our angelic customer. If we sell in a start-up situation, we can examine the best customers of a competing or similar business. Angelic customers should be spending money at a minimum dollar level or possess the economic profile that allows them to purchase our product. There should also be a high probability that they will buy again, offer a strong recommendation, or offer other benefits that make interacting with them righteously satisfying.

To uncover the information needed to create the angelic customer profile, we need to analyze our sales reports and scrutinize customer surveys, whether they were done formally or informally. We should factor in all available market research and data as we begin to conceptualize our angelic customer. If such resources are not available, you'll have to rely on your intellect and experience. You should also consult with others that you deem knowledgeable about your industry and selling. Jesus recruited Matthew, a tax collector with research and record-keeping skills, for heavenly purposes. Someone in another department such as accounting or marketing may be able to assist you in creating your angelic customer profile (see Matthew 9:9–13). Of course, as people selling God's way, this entire project must be brought before the Lord in prayer. Through praying, you will seek and receive godly wisdom and guidance from the Holy Spirit.

The Angelic Customer Profile

The angelic customer profile is a detailed description of all the common characteristics and attributes of our very best potential customers; building this profile is vital to prospecting successfully. For businesses needing a consistent cycle of repeat sales from a collection of core customers, creating an angelic customer profile starts by determining the minimum amount of money a customer needs to spend in a year to earn a place on the angelic customer list. This minimum dollar level can be found by ranking all customers by dollars spent within the past year, starting from highest to lowest.

Then start with the customer at the top of the list, the biggest spender, and list the revenue spent by each customer in descending order, ending with the customer whose inclusion makes the total number 80 percent of the total yearly revenue. Logically, this requires that we know our yearly revenue total and calculate 80 percent of that number first. The amount of money spent by the last customer counted becomes the minimum dollar level. This is sometimes called the "80-20 Rule." Eighty percent of a company's revenue typically comes from 20 percent of its customers.

In sales that typically involve one-time transactions, like real estate, insurance, and investments, creating the angelic customer profile starts by summarizing what's needed economically for a prospect to purchase our product or service. We look at factors such as household income, debt ratios, employment history, and credit scores. The angelic profile for this type of prospect may include features such as having a credit score of 700, $10,000 in investable assets, and homeownership for the previous ten years. While prospecting, we may need a prospect's permission to obtain credit reports or bank account information. This allows us to dig very deep, hoping to find anything of significance that allows us to qualify a prospect as a legitimate potential buyer. Once we confirm their legitimacy, we add them to our list of target prospects. These types of prospects will probably purchase once, and then it may be years or even decades before they'll have a need for our services. But these customers can be an excellent source for referrals and positive reviews.

Future Sales and Recommendations

Our angelic customers must have one or both of the following attributes: a high probability for future recurring sales or a high probability to deliver referrals that lead to sales. In analyzing a customer's potential for future sales, we look at their economic profile, current financial status, and proclivity for personal or business growth. This will give us insights into their buying behavior and help us determine whether they will continually need what we sell. If the prospect appears to be financially sound, operates in a sustainable industry, and has a growth mindset, we know we have a prospect with a high probability for future sales, especially in business-to-business selling scenarios.

In analyzing a customer's potential for a strong referral or recommendation, we look at the results of their formal and informal customer satisfaction surveys. Satisfaction surveys give us insights into a customer's probability for a referral. These surveys can be completed informally or formally. It's always important to question customers to find areas of fulfillment and frustration as it relates to what we sell and how we sell it. Any significant information we acquire about our best customers empowers us as we approach other prospects, because we know prospects with a profile and mindset like that of our angelic customers have a strong probability of becoming satisfied customers.

Creating Lists

After you determine the minimum dollar level a potential prospect needs to spend to be considered an "angelic customer," the next step is to construct a list of your customers who already belong in that category. This is a list of companies and people that you want to repeatedly buy again, or this is a list of current customers that you hope will provide positive reviews and recommendations. If your business needs a consistent cycle of repeat sales from a core group of customers, you should compile a list that includes all your current customers who spent above the minimum dollar level within the past year. These customers have a high probability for future sales because of the satisfaction they expressed about your service.

If your business typically needs one sales transaction per customer per year, you should compile a list of current customers who spent at or above the minimum dollar level and who have a high probability for making positive recommendations. The customers on these lists also need to exhibit a level of righteousness that makes selling to them satisfying for your company.

This is your angelic customer list; it is the basis for creating a written profile of your angelic customer. As I stated earlier, the angelic customer profile describes the attributes and characteristics common to all customers on the angelic customer list. The next section provides sixty areas to investigate in creating a profile of your angelic customer. Although some areas may not be relevant, the lists in this chapter can help in creating descriptive profiles of angelic customers. The profile needs to be posted as a visible reminder of what makes a great prospect. Your list of target prospects will be drawn out of the angelic customer profile; therefore, it's wise to examine the angelic customer profile and update it every year.

If you are in a start-up mode and no customer base exists, then you must create an angelic customer profile based upon the sixty areas below and any information that you can find through extensive research. If you are in a selling environment where sales are predominantly transactional and you do not have a working list of customers, then you need to visually inspect and verbally question customers considering the sixty areas below. The latter scenario most often occurs in retail selling environments.

Analyze Your Best Customers

An examination of our best customers helps us create a written description of our angelic customer. This is our "Angelic Customer Profile."

Demographics

- Years in business
- Number of employees
- Number of locations
- Competitors
- Incomes
- Gender
- Ages
- Occupation
- Geography
- Educational profile
- Personnel backgrounds
- Products and services
- Decision-makers
- Technology
- Vendors
- Demographic rankings
- Marital status
- Family Structure

Economics

- Annual revenue
- Industry trends
- Stock price
- Profit margins
- Pricing
- Salaries
- Credit score
- Debt
- Economic history
- Buying processes
- Industry ratings
- Marketing/advertising
- Purchasing history
- Cost of sale
- Selling process
- Budgets
- Problem solving
- Buying habits
- Incomes
- Problems
- Opportunities
- Education
- Website
- Press releases

Psychographics

- Religious beliefs
- Executives' accessibility
- Available agents or representatives
- News stories
- Recruitment efforts
- Customer service
- Own vs. rent
- Mission statements
- Work styles
- Vision statements
- After work lifestyle
- Work ethic
- Growth plans
- Negotiating tactics
- Community involvement
- Emotional factors
- Crisis behavior
- Resolution skills

I'll include an example of an angelic customer profile later in this chapter. However, the next step is to develop the prospect list by finding potential buyers with the same characteristics of those found in your angelic customer profile. We find potential buyers worthy of inclusion by investigating websites, past customers, social networks, walk-in traffic, discarded files, gatekeepers, company reports, business associates, friends, phone inquiries, news stories, all types of media, all forms of advertising, and request for proposals. We need to analyze all possible resources to find important people, titles, phone numbers, and addresses. We'll need this information because the next step is to arrange meetings with any decision-maker who can influence buying what we sell.

When we find a prospect with similar attributes and characteristics of those in our angelic profile, then we have a possible buyer with the potential of becoming an angelic customer. As wise sellers, we need to spend most of our prospecting time with these people and companies. Yes, this also means we may need to spend significant time digging deep within a specific company to find and connect with one targeted person.

It takes time in the qualifying stage before any of us can determine whether a prospect truly possesses the characteristics of an angelic customer. The important thing is to find potential buyers who appear to have the characteristics of an angelic customer and put them on the list of target prospects.

Goal Two: Meetings

As we create our list of target prospects, we need to arrange meetings. This is the second goal in digging deep. Like the wise builder who arranges meetings with different people and companies before the building begins. We often need to employ a combination of phone calls, mailings, marketing campaigns, or walk-ins to get meetings. Being diligent is very important, because even wise builders encounter delays in construction projects. Deterrents such as unreturned phone calls or an administrative assistant blocking access to a decision-maker must not diminish our determination. We need meetings to take place face-to-face, phone-to-phone, or computer-to-computer regardless of whether a potential buyer finds us through our company's marketing efforts or we find a potential buyer through prospecting: As wise sellers, we need a significant number of meetings.

In some scenarios, we need meetings with several decision-makers in an organization. Sometimes, when there are several decision-makers, it might not be possible to meet with everyone. However, we do need to meet with at least one decision-maker empowered with significant influence. That person can help us understand the needs and roles of all the other decision-makers, like the wise builder who needs at least one person to communicate with while building a house to make it a home.

We Need Meetings

Once we have our list of target prospects, we need meetings. We need meetings to take place face-to-face, phone-to-phone, or computer-to-computer.

Goal Three: Qualifying

Qualifying prospects is the third goal in the digging-deep process. We look beyond appearances to assess a prospect's true potential for becoming an angelic customer, like the wise builder who inspects the structure's foundation to determine its durability. We're qualifying to determine a prospect's viability for significant revenue and a righteous relationship.

Prepare Greetings

As we connect with prospects, we need to give them our greeting. This means we prepare honest and inviting greetings.

It's best to use a system to rate or rank prospects before and after the first meeting. Before the first meeting, the ranking or rating helps us assign a priority to the prospect. After the first meeting, it's a good idea to reprioritize a prospect. The first meeting provides the initial opportunity to verify the information gathered while digging deep. Through qualifying, I've often discovered that a prospect thought to be average with a low priority is a great prospect with a high priority.

You can use an alphabetic or numeric code or some combination to rank or rate prospects. For example, prospects can be prioritized alphabetically, graded in comparison to clients in the angelic customer profile. The prospect who possesses 90 to 100 percent of the angelic customer's characteristics gets an A; 80 to 90 percent, a B; 70 to 80 percent, a C; 60 to 70 percent, a D; and below 60 percent, an F.

Prospects can also be ranked by assigning numerical values to their attributes as they are found in the angelic customer profile. The numerical scale could go from one to one hundred. For example, our angelic customer profile could describe our best customers as being corporations that have been in business for at least ten years, conduct business internationally, and have over $50 million in annual revenue. The angelic customer profile includes ten additional qualities that aren't as important as the first three. A prospect could be assigned ten points for each of the top three characteristics they have and three points for each additional attribute.

For example, a prospect could get ten points for conducting business internationally and ten points for operating with over $50 million in annual revenue. They could get an additional twenty-one points for having seven of the least important qualities, making this hypothetical prospect's total score forty-one. Prospects who score the highest are assigned top priority. Later in this chapter, I'll explain an example that uses both letters and numbers.

Search for Someone Worthy

> *Whatever town or village you enter, search for some worthy person there and stay at his house until you leave. As you enter the home, give it your greeting. If the home is deserving let your peace rest on it; if it is not, let your peace return to you. If anyone will not welcome you or listen to your words, leave that home or town and shake the dust off your feet.*
>
> —Matthew 10:11–14

In the Gospel of Matthew, Jesus sent out His disciples to gather prospects for the kingdom of God. The instructions He gave more than two thousand years ago still apply today, not only for taking people through a process of spiritual growth, but also for taking prospects through the sales process. Jesus instructed His disciples to search for someone worthy. He gave them the responsibility of reaching out to people who appeared to be ideal candidates for Christianity; likewise, we should reach out to prospects who appear to have the potential to become angelic customers.

As we connect with prospects, we need to give them our greeting, just as Jesus instructed His disciples: "*As you enter the home, give it your greeting. If the home is deserving, let your peace rest on it; if it is not, let your peace return to you*" (Matthew 10:12–13). Jesus's instructions should motivate us to prepare an honest, inviting, and revealing greeting for each prospect. It's a way of letting our peace rest on a situation. Being truthful and transparent, we fully identify ourselves, our company, and our purpose. Some companies cloak themselves and what they're selling while prospecting; this type of deception goes against the basic principles of doing anything God's way.

In our greeting, we should communicate an understanding of the prospect's needs, and our reasons for a meeting should center on the prospect's priorities. We can include questions in our greeting as we seek to gain a greater understanding of a prospect's needs. Our invitation to meet must provide the prospect with a simple way to say yes or no. We motivate, not manipulate, to get meetings.

Not everyone will be open to what we offer; we are only reaching out to people who appear to be ideal potential prospects.

We will find out if they meet the criteria for being an angelic customer once we uncover their wants and needs. It's important to deliver our greeting and ask questions in a manner that lays a foundation for a relationship built on biblical principles of honesty and righteousness.

Sometimes, honesty and righteousness may lead to a prospect's rejecting what we offer, leaving us feeling dejected and discouraged. The disciples dealt with numerous people who rejected the salvation offered through Jesus Christ. We need to do as Jesus instructed the disciples to do in situations where they were rejected. We need to shake the dust off and discard the rejection, press on through any discouragement and its negative residue, and then leave that prospect.

2000-Year-Old Wisdom

The instructions Jesus gave more than two thousand years ago still apply today, not only for taking people through a process of spiritual growth, but also for taking prospects through a sales process.

Search for Someone Worthy While Selling Advertising

As I stated earlier in this chapter, prospecting begins by what I call "digging deep," which is a process of searching through an immense amount of information and contacting numerous people after we have created our angelic customer profile. I also stated that digging deep has three goals. The first goal is to develop a list of prospects based upon our angelic customer profile. For example, while selling radio advertising time, I created a list of prospects, by first fully comprehending the radio station's angelic customer profile. The last radio station I worked for was WAVA, a Christian teaching and talk radio station in the Washington, DC, market. For WAVA, the following served as the angelic customer profile:

> A WAVA angelic customer spends at least $72,000 within a twelve-month period. The customer advertises throughout the entire metro area. Their target market matches our WAVA audience demographically. The customer believes mass marketing provides a way to avoid problems and grow their business. One or several of the decision-makers at the company can discuss expectations and come to an agreement about the potential results of an advertising campaign. A decision-maker possessing significant influence is accessible, typically the decision-maker with final authority regarding how money is spent. One or more of the decision-makers is a Christian or at least communicates Christian values.

Using this profile as a guide, I compiled a list of prospects by listening to other radio stations, scanning direct mail pieces, reading newspapers, watching TV, scouring websites, and getting referrals from customers. As a result of the radio station's marketing efforts, the list also included prospects who called the radio station inquiring about advertising. I eliminated a significant number of companies, because of their apparent lack of angelic customer characteristics.

As I compiled my list of prospects, I moved into the second goal of digging deep: arranging meetings. I began making phone calls, sending emails, and walking into offices with targeted invitations and marketing brochures. My efforts ended with a request for a meeting with a decision-maker. Of course, being diligent was very important. I could not let unreturned phone calls or an administrative assistant blocking access to a decision-maker diminish my determination. To sell advertising successfully, I needed meetings to take place face-to-face, phone-to-phone, or computer-to-computer. In some scenarios, I needed meetings with several decision-makers. Sometimes, I pursued prospects for months before securing the first meeting. I always attempted to secure the first meeting with ideas for campaigns that centered on the prospect's needs. All the companies I approached needed new customers or former customers to return as prospects. Their specific advertising needs lay in what prevented or motivated their prospects to become new or returning customers.

The third goal in digging deep and searching for someone worthy is qualifying, which must be ongoing because a prospect's circumstances and financial situation may change. Qualifying requires us to determine the prospect's potential to become a satisfied angelic customer. In qualifying prospects at WAVA, I used a grading system that assigned a number to each of the seven areas of the angelic customer profile. The maximum score a prospect could get was seventy because each of the seven areas had a maximum value of ten. After scoring a prospect, I assigned a grade that reflected the prospect's potential for becoming an angelic customer.

In the following scoring example, the prospect initially received an average grade (C), but this prospect ultimately became a great customer. In selling God's way, we can work with subpar prospects, interact with them in righteous ways, and turn a questionable prospect into a satisfied angelic customer. The important thing is to dig deep (prospect thoroughly), and then take the foundation (the right type of potential customer), and lay it on the Word of God, biblical principles (see John 1:1–2).

Example of Qualifying

Prospect: An automobile dealership that specialized in selling new American-made luxury sedans. Each category received a score from one to ten, with one being the worst and ten being best:

- Ability to spend at least $72,000 on radio advertising in one year. *Score*: 5
- Geographic market includes the entire Washington, DC, metropolitan area. *Score*: 3
- Target market matches station's audience demographically. *Score*: 7
- Company trying to avoid problems or grow through marketing. *Score*: 2
- Prospect able to discuss advertising expectations and come to an agreement about results. *Score*: 10
- The decision-makers are accessible for meetings, especially the person with the final authority regarding expenditures. *Score*: 10
- One or several of the decision-makers are Christian or at least appear to embrace Christian ethics. *Score*: 10

Total score: 47 points

Grading System:

- Score between 70 and 60: High Priority (A)
- Score between 59 and 50: Secondary Priority (B)
- Score between 49 and 40: Low Priority (C)
- Score between 39 and 30: No Priority (D)
- Score between 29 and 20: Dismiss (F)

An A represented a good-to-great prospect; B, an above-average prospect; C, an average prospect; D, a below-average prospect; and F, a prospect not worth pursuing. Any prospect with a score below 40 was not worth pursuing. The A and B prospects received the most time and attention.

Delivering the Greeting

In prospecting at WAVA radio, I often greeted prospects by saying: "My name is Michael Hamer. I'm with WAVA, the Christian teaching and talk radio station." After my introduction, I often said, "The reason I'm calling (or stopping by or emailing) is to set up an appointment with the person in charge of advertising."

I always wanted people to quickly understand who I was and my purpose for contacting them. From that point on in the conversation, I communicated reasons why that company should want to have a meeting with me. These reasons often revolved around a campaign idea, success story, or statistics that validated my ability to serve. For example, in approaching a car dealer in the suburbs of Washington, DC, I stated that almost 100 percent of our listeners were suburban homeowners, who preferred American-made cars. In approaching an ice cream retail operation, I suggested a campaign idea that involved promoting ice cream sundaes at churches.

Preparing a proper greeting requires completing enough research to attain a basic understanding of a prospect's priorities. I ended my greetings by inviting prospects to meet at a time convenient for them. If a prospect accepted my greeting, then I proceeded through the sales process. If a prospect was not accepting, then I proceeded to the next potential buyer. Regardless of the prospect's response, I continued to pursue my goals, not harboring any bitterness or embracing discouragement, but learning from my mistakes (and in some cases forgetting the rejection that just occurred). We can't change history, but we can affect the future. Focus your efforts on the prospects at hand and those ahead of you, not on those behind you.

Rejection most often occurs in the prospecting stage; while it should not be taken personally, any sort of rejection can feel impersonal, disappointing, and unkind. We are often rejected for legitimate reasons, such as there is no budget to buy what we are selling. At other times, we may be rejected by a person who is misinformed or rude. We may say and do all the right things while prospecting and still get rejected for some unknown reason. Whenever we experience the discouragement of rejection, we should identify ourselves as beloved children of God, empowered with ways and goals that are justifiable and righteous. In the book of Philippians, Paul talks about forgetting what's behind and working toward receiving all that Christ promises.

As we strive to sell God's way, we should incorporate Paul's attitude about forgetting the past and moving on, maximizing our incomes and business relationships as we bring glory to

God by being followers of our Lord and Savior, Jesus Christ (see Philippians 3:12–14).

Work Forward

Tell yourself: "Regardless of the prospect's response, I'm proceeding forward, not harboring any bitterness, but learning from mistakes (and, in some cases, forgetting things that just occurred)." We need to focus our efforts on the prospects at hand, and those ahead of us, not on those behind us. We can't change history, but we can affect the future.

Transition to Questions and not Presentations

I've observed far too many salespeople err by jumping right into a presentation after delivering their greeting because they sensed that they have found someone worthy. I too have made that same mistake. However, what is needed at this point in the process, if the prospect accepts our greeting, is patience. We must patiently and politely transition into asking even more questions.

There are several places in the Bible where Jesus dealt with a problem or opportunity by first asking questions. In Matthew 16:13–17, Jesus questioned the disciples about who He was. Peter answered that it was clear Jesus was the Messiah, the Son of the living God. In John 4:7–9, Jesus asked a woman at a well if she would give Him a drink. He went on to present a solution that would save her soul and allow her to never thirst again.

Even when a prospect approaches us, the questioning stage must be completed before a presentation is made. In Mark 10:35–36, the disciples approached Jesus about the opportunity to be great. He responded to their questions with more questions, after which He presented a solution that offered everyone the opportunity to be great by becoming servants. Jesus told them the person who served all would be the greatest. Questioning God's way always leads to glorious presentations. I believe asking a righteous question is one of the most powerful things we can do while selling.

Questions

1. Are you satisfied that your angelic customer profile is a well-written description of your best customers?

2. Are prospecting greetings filled with truth and transparency? Do those greetings make it easy for a prospect to quickly understand who your company is and what you sell?

3. What are the three most important things that you must do to obtain meetings with your prospects?

4. How do you deal with rejection? Have you found a way to become encouraged and empowered after being rejected?

Scriptural References

- Digging deep to lay a foundation is important in prospecting:

  They are *like a man building a house, who dug down deep and laid the foundation on rock. When a flood came, the torrent struck that house but could not shake it, because it was well built. But the one who hears my words and does not put them into practice is like a man who built a house on the ground without a foundation. The moment the torrent struck that house, it collapsed and its destruction was complete* (Luke 6:48–49).

- The Word of God stands forever. Biblical wisdom is righteous for eternity:

  The word of the Lord endures forever. And this is the word that was preached to you (1 Peter 1:25).

- We need to be mindful of the people and prospects we associate with:

  Do not give dogs what is sacred; do not throw your pearls to pigs. If you do, they may trample them under their feet, and turn and tear you to pieces (Matthew 7:6).

  Do not be misled: Bad company corrupts good character (1 Corinthians 15:33).

- The Great Commission shows us the importance of prospecting:

  Then Jesus came to them and said, "All authority in heaven and on earth has been given to me. Therefore go and make disciples of all nations, baptizing them in the name of the Father and of the Son and of the Holy Spirit" (Matthew 28:18–19).

- Jesus recruited Matthew, a tax collector with research and record-keeping skills, for heavenly purposes:

  As Jesus went on from there, he saw a man named Matthew sitting at the tax collector's booth. "Follow me," he told him, and Matthew got up and followed him. While Jesus was having dinner at Matthew's house, many tax collectors and sinners came and ate with him and his disciples. When the Pharisees saw this, they asked his disciples, "Why does your teacher eat with tax collectors and sinners?" On hearing this, Jesus said, "It is not the healthy who need a doctor, but the sick. But go and learn what this means: 'I desire mercy, not sacrifice.' For I have not come to call the righteous, but sinners" (Matthew 9:9–13).

- Jesus is the Word in flesh, our rock, and our foundation:

  In the beginning was the Word, and the Word was with God, and the Word was God. He was with God in the beginning (John 1:1–2).

- Jesus's instructions on prospecting for souls are useful in prospecting for customers:

  Whatever town or village you enter, search for some worthy person there and stay at his house until you leave. As you enter the home, give it your greeting. If the home is deserving let your peace rest on it; if it is not, let your peace return to you. If anyone will not welcome you or listen to your words, leave that home or town and shake the dust off your feet (Matthew 10:11–14).

- Paul talks about forgetting what's behind and straining toward the goal. We should adopt this same attitude while prospecting:

  Not that I have already obtained all this, or have already been made perfect, but I press on to take hold of that for which Christ Jesus took hold of me. Brothers and sisters, I do not consider myself yet to have taken hold of it. But one thing I do: Forgetting what is behind and straining toward what is ahead, I press on toward the goal to win the prize for which God has called me heavenward in Christ Jesus (Philippians 3:12–14).

- Jesus asked questions before presenting the truth about His church. Asking righteous questions before making a presentation paves the way to more powerful revelations:

  When Jesus came to the region of Caesarea Philippi, he asked his disciples, "Who do people say the Son of Man is?" They replied, "Some say John the Baptist; others say

Elijah; and still others, Jeremiah or one of the prophets." "But what about you?" he asked. "Who do you say I am?" Simon Peter answered, "You are the Messiah the Son of the living God" (Matthew 16:13–16).

- Jesus questioned a Samaritan woman before presenting her with a life-changing solution. We should imitate Jesus while selling and question righteously before presenting solutions:

  When a Samaritan woman came to draw water, Jesus said to her, "Will you give me a drink?" (His disciples had gone into the town to buy food.) The Samaritan woman said to him, "You are a Jew and I am a Samaritan woman. How can you ask me for a drink" (For Jews do not associate with Samaritans.) (John 4:7–9).

- Jesus responds to two disciples' question with a question of His own before presenting a glorious opportunity. We can politely answer a question by asking questions before we present a solution or opportunity. It's our way of setting the stage to present something in a more noteworthy context:

  Then James and John, the sons of Zebedee, came to him. "Teacher," they said, "we want you to do for us whatever we ask." "What do you want me to do for you?" he asked (Mark 10:35–36).

CHAPTER 6:

The Questions

But the L*ORD* *God called to the man, "Where are you?" He answered, "I heard you in the garden, and I was afraid because I was naked; so I hid." And he said, "Who told you that you were naked? Have you eaten from the tree that I commanded you not to eat from?" The man said, "The woman you put here with me—she gave me some fruit from the tree, and I ate it." Then the Lord God said to the woman, "What is this you have done?" The woman said, "The serpent deceived me, and I ate."*

—Genesis 3:9–13

Adam and Eve Questioned

In this powerful story, which occurs near the beginning of creation, God questions Adam about his sin. Adam's sin presented a massive problem, because it allowed sin to enter the world for the entire human race. Fortunately for us, God provided a solution.

Questioning is arguably the most important stage in the sales process. It's often referred to as the needs analysis, sales interview, or consultation. Questioning reveals problems and opportunities. With problems and opportunities comes a need for what we sell. Asking questions is the most powerful thing we can do while selling. If we question correctly, the people we question will have a learning experience. Their answers will reveal or confirm truths—facts about their own disposition, character, and circumstances—not only to us, but to them as well.

There are two goals in questioning. The first is to gather information that reveals needs that are important and urgent, requiring immediate action to solve a problem or maximize an opportunity. The second goal, which can be accomplished simultaneously, is the construction of a righteous relationship. Our goal as righteous sellers is not to close sales, but to open relationships that generate sales.

Most Important

Questioning is arguably the most important stage in the sales process. It's often referred to as the needs analysis, sales interview, or consultation. Questioning reveals problems and opportunities. With problems and opportunities come needs for what we sell.

Gathering Information

The questioning stage starts by verifying the basics. In the previous stage (prospecting), we uncovered the basic information as it pertains to who a prospect is and their current circumstances. So, we should know most of these answers before asking the basic questions.

According to the Bible, the first question God ever asked anyone was when He asked Adam, "*Where are you?*" God knew Adam's answer before He asked the question. I believe God asked Adam this question so that Adam would have a learning experience and look at his situation realistically, seeing the sin he and Eve had committed and realizing the consequences. Previously, in Genesis 2:17, God told Adam if he ate from the tree of knowledge, he would die. So, Adam knew that he had committed a sin and that death would surely follow; He also perceived that God knew as well. As salespeople, we ask who, what, where, and when questions to verify the basic information about our prospect, confirming information that we gathered doing our research. We ask these questions because we may need prospects to have a learning or confirming experience, as they realize their own wants, needs, and dispositions.

After the basic questions, we probe into areas where we sense problems or opportunities. Problems come connected to answers that express fears, frustrations, and dissatisfactions. Opportunities come attached to answers that express eagerness, dreams, and goals. So, in getting answers to the basic questions, we want prospects to express their emotions and motivations as they communicate opinions and facts. In answering God, Adam expressed fear because of his nakedness and stated that this motivated him to hide. If prospects are not expressing emotions and motivations, or if we surmise that we're not getting information about their need for immediate action, then our next set of questions should uncover whether a prospect truly needs what we sell. Very pointed what and why questions work best at this point. We are questioning to find out exactly what's needed and why it's needed. It is perfectly OK to ask a prospect, "What type of product are you hoping to buy and why?"

Next, God asked Adam, "*Who told you that you were naked?*" God's follow-up questions probed into areas that would reveal other people. As wise sellers, we question to uncover all decision-makers and people of influence. God proceeded to ask, "*Have you eaten from the tree that I commanded you not to eat from?*" This question allowed the full extent of the problem to be known.

We need to agree with prospects about the severity of a problem or the magnitude of an opportunity. "Did you . . .?" or "Have you . . .?" questions work best here. As people selling God's way, we're attempting to probe the past while analyzing current conditions and personal preferences related to what we sell. We do this to ascertain the proper perspective on the size of the current problem or opportunity. What a prospect did in the past to solve a problem or maximize an opportunity or their current efforts to address their needs and goals gives us insight into the magnitude of their desires. If they are currently doing nothing or very little to find solutions or advantage opportunities, then they are not assigning a high priority to what we are discussing. As righteous sellers, we'll have to ask questions that gently probe into why they are doing nothing or very little to solve their problem or take advantage of an opportunity.

The size of the solution (what we sell) directly equates to the size of the opportunity. How long have they needed our solution? What will happen if they don't seize our solution? These answers give us insight into exactly how much of what we offer is needed and how soon it's needed. Since Adam's sin was so severe, leading to his inevitable his death, a massive solution was needed immediately.

Next, God questioned the woman, the other person involved in the sin. He asked Eve, "*What is this you have done?*" As wise salespeople, we should question, if possible, all the people who influence the buying decision. We need a complete understanding of the prospect's buying process. We can go through the sales process efficiently if we have a complete understanding of a prospect's buying process. After God completed His questioning, He immediately presented assignments to Adam, Eve, and the serpent as visions of their future. Their assignments, which needed to begin immediately, provided a solution to the sin problem.

Once we gather enough of the right type of information, we can present a solution that solves their problem or an opportunity that advantages their situation. Because we believe that the prospect holds an accurate perspective regarding their needs and urgency for what we're selling. Additionally, it reflects our understanding of the prospect's buying process (i.e., how they decide to buy what we're selling, their thoughts and behavior from start to finish, and the emotions they experience while buying something that we sell). The solution or opportunity that we present should come wrapped in a vision of the future.

A Prospect's Buying Process

Understand the prospect's buying process and behavior from start to finish, along with the emotions they experience while buying something we sell.

Assignments

The assignment focuses on the solution needed. Assignments are actions steps that must be completed by an agreed-upon deadline. Assignments often include action steps that must be completed by the prospect and the salesperson, within a specified time frame. After questioning, we must agree with the prospect about the next steps in the sales process. The assignment clarifies the next steps. If it's a presentation, then we need to agree with the prospect about what needs to be presented, how it needs to be presented, when it needs to be presented, and most importantly, why it needs to be presented. The assignment helps to solidify the relationship because it's a contract for action. All this should be discussed during the questioning; this helps to set the stage for the buying commitment that we ask for during our close.

Not all assignments are fulfilled. For a variety of reasons, people may fail to complete an assignment. I've given prospects the assignment of securing funds they thought were available, only to discover those funds were no longer accessible. Later, I may question this same prospect and give another assignment, especially if the prospect operates within righteous principles. Incomplete assignments should not discourage us from making more assignments, because a completed assignment accompanies a high probability of sales success (see Galatians 6:9–10 and James 2:17).

When selling advertising, I could predict the prospect's likelihood to buy through the depth of the agreed-upon assignment. The more components of an assignment, the more committed prospects were to buying. Here's an example of an in-depth assignment: A prospect agrees to see a presentation for an exact dollar amount, by a specified date in a certain format.

In addition, I committed to producing a sample commercial that the prospect can hear before the presentation. The prospect committed to get me the information for the sample commercial by close of business the next day. And they committed to secure the funding , while making sure others within the company will attend the presentation.

Solutions

The solution is what we sell, customized to meet specific needs or take advantage of time-sensitive opportunities. During the questioning stage of the sales process, we must summarize the solution we plan on presenting. The complete solution with details arrives during the presentation, the next stage in the sales process. If enacted, the solution affects the future, so our summary must include a vision of the future with our solution in place. The summarized solution God gave Adam, Eve, and the serpent, included customized visions of their futures. Everyone knew what to expect. The serpent (Satan) would be crushed by one of Eve's offspring (Jesus). Adam could no longer live in paradise, a place where he did not have to work strenuously for survival. He would be forced to live in a world where surviving required arduous work. Eve could no longer live in paradise, a place where God created people. She would have to live in a world where giving birth to offspring would require severe pain (see Genesis 3:14–20).

A solution can be presented with, or without, the prospect's permission. Immediately after questioning Adam and Eve, God presented a solution that required them to buy into living differently if they wanted to continue existing. This shows us that we do not need permission from a prospect to present a solution. However, we're not God, so we're more likely to get a sale if we get a prospect's cooperation in our quest to present solutions. Prospects cooperate by answering and asking questions. In most cases, prospects do cooperate, because we're attempting to solve their problem or take advantage of their opportunity. At this point in the sales process, they also believe we can solve problems and maximize opportunities. If they didn't hold this belief, their cooperation would have ceased during the asking of basic questions.

Expectations

Discussing all the possible outcomes during the questioning stage helps in establishing credibility and dependability. This is vital for constructing righteous relationships. Having agreed upon expectations before a prospect buys contributes to customer satisfaction. Repeat contracts and referrals come from satisfied customers. If we wait until after a prospect buys to discuss expectations, then we may discover they expected something that is not likely to happen or that the results received are not the results desired. This opens the door to customer dissatisfaction as expectations and needs go unfulfilled. For salespeople, customer dissatisfaction leads to declining incomes and destructive relationships.

Here are two examples from my years selling advertising in which the results of a client's campaign were unpredictable:

- A furniture store client advertised for weeks they were having a sale on sofas, and a significant number of new people came into the store. But no one bought a sofa, leaving my client with a large stock of unsold sofas and hard-to-define results.

- An automobile client launched an advertising campaign connected to a special financing offer. This same ad campaign and offer had worked well for similar car dealers countless times in capturing customers. However, this time, the ad campaign yielded negative results because a competitor with a better financing offer advertised at the same time.

In both these examples, I needed to first have enough product knowledge to explain the results of advertising on any radio station. Second, I needed to bring up the topic of expectations during the questioning stage of the sales process. This allowed me to discuss all possibilities and ensure the prospects knew exactly what to expect when they bought advertising from the radio station I represented.

A great deal of my success selling advertising hinged on the outcome of the discussion about expectations. As I stated earlier, the potential outcome of a client's advertising campaign was often unpredictable. What I knew for certain were the facts associated with the station's audience and technical capabilities. So, I needed to help clients understand that they could have high expectations about the station's ability to deliver their message to the audience even though the results of their advertising could not be easily defined. With this understanding we could agree about expected results while instilling honesty and wisdom in our relationship. This helped establish me as a salesperson, selling righteously, who could be trusted in future sales transactions.

In both examples above, I continued to do business with these clients because they benefited from advertising with the radio station I represented. They found value in delivering their advertising message to a significant number of people who could potentially purchase or influence a purchase of their products, which was the expected benefit that I discussed.

Building and Maintaining Relationships

> *Finally, all of you, be like-minded, be sympathetic, love one another, be compassionate and humble. Do not repay evil with evil or insult with insult. On the contrary, repay evil with blessing, because to this you were called so that you may inherit a blessing. For,*
>
> *"Whoever would love life and see good days must keep their tongue from evil and their lips from deceitful speech. They must turn from evil and do good, they must seek peace and pursue it."*
>
> —1 Peter 3:8–11

More than two thousand years ago, Peter, a disciple of Jesus, gave us instructions for building and maintaining righteous relationships. These are the same principles we should employ today as we move through the sales process. In this stage of the sales process, we begin to invest significant time with a prospect, hopefully meeting face-to-face. In the prospecting stage, we begin laying the foundation for a righteous relationship. In the questioning stage, we get entrenched in building that relationship. There are five areas we commit to building to construct righteous relationships. If we can successfully build these areas during the questioning stage, we'll establish ways of interacting that work wonderfully throughout the entire sales process and for future interactions with this person. The five areas we commit to build in are truth and transparency, common connections, comfortable chats, care-filled confrontations, and empathetic evaluations.

Constructing Righteous Relationships?
Build in These Five Areas

1. Truth and Transparency
2. Common Connections
3. Comfortable Chats
4. Care-filled Confrontations
5. Empathetic Evaluations

Constructing compassionate, caring, compatible, comfortable, and truth-filled, relationships with people does not require that they be compassionate, caring, compatible, comfortable, and truthful with us. As people selling God's way, we can build in these areas without the prospect's cooperation. The Bible instructs us to love our enemies, and to treat others like we want them to treat us (see Luke 6:27–31).

Truth and Transparency

If your selling style is not soaked in truth and transparency, then you are ruining your potential for positive customer reviews, referrals, and repeat purchases. As people selling righteously, we must exclude lies and deceit from our sales processes, especially if we are communicating or implying an end-result that we cannot guarantee. We need to embrace total truth and transparency and not withhold any information that could be considered vital to a prospect's buying process. We need to discuss any flawed research presented or data that cannot be fully substantiated as valid. It is also important to clearly explain any technical problems that could occur and present proactive technical solutions. If aspects of what we sell contain the possibility of negatively impacting a prospect, then we need to bring those things into the light (discussion) and not hide anything potentially destructive to a prospect or client (see Mark 4:21–22 and Ephesians 4:25).

The Bible instructs us in several places to avoid lies and deceit, but not only should we hold this standard for ourselves, we should encourage others to do so as well. Genesis 3 describes Adam sinning and then hiding. It's God who takes the initiative and approaches Adam to question him. If we sense that a prospect is hiding issues or aspects of their situation, then we need to probe those areas to bring truth and transparency into the relationship. We need accurate information to offer appropriate solutions. If we try to produce solutions with incomplete or inaccurate information, then the quality of our solution suffers. This makes the probability of closing a sale and opening a righteous relationship unlikely.

Here is an example from my days in the radio industry, where I encountered prospects hiding the fact that there were other decision-makers, besides themselves, allowing me to continue the sales process without knowing the perspective of all the decision-makers. These situations often led to frustration and not a sale, since the solution I presented did not address the needs of all the decision-makers. At other times, salespeople presented aspects of what they sold without approval from a manager, to offer that specific solution being discussed. The prospect would often rejoice in anticipation of a much-needed solution. However, this excitement was replaced with displeasure because the solution expected never arrived.

In both cases, the sales processes ended in dissatisfaction because of a lack of transparency and truth. If the prospect had told me that no solution could be presented without input from other key decision-makers, then my next step would have been to arrange a meeting with those people instead of wasting time developing an unsellable solution. In the second example, if the salesperson had told the prospect they did not have the authority to offer the solution as discussed, then the prospect could have withheld their glee until approval arrived.

Bringing all the issues into the light decreases the number of potential sales ending in dissatisfaction. Truth and transparency give all parties an exact understanding about the next step in the sales process, and it also infuses integrity into the business relationship. The lack of truth and transparency allows lies and deceit to demolish sales processes, relationships, incomes, and careers.

Be Transparent

Truth and transparency give all parties an exact understanding about the next step in the sales process.

Common Connections

We should question prospects in ways that build upon the things we have in common, the shared values, experiences, and relationships. Adam was made in the image of God and was the first person to share an intimate relationship with Him. They shared a valuable connection that allowed God to question, correct, and serve him intimately. A person's cooperation increases if they sense they're working with someone who shares their background and values. Chapter 3 of 1Peter encourages us to be of one mind in relationships. This means we need to search for and build upon significant commonalities.

To find and build upon these common connections, we must go beyond routine topics like children, camping, and card games. We need to discuss principles and belief systems behind answers. We need to ask lots of "how" and "why" questions, to gain a greater understanding of the prospect's or company's ideology. Examples of questions could be: "How did you come to that conclusion?" "Why does this situation exist?" If we ask enough of these types of questions, we can connect with better prospects more effectively or separate from poor prospects more efficiently. For example, if the prospect operates in ways compatible with Christian beliefs, then they are essentially telling us to sell and behave righteously, because they value things like integrity and accountability. Of course, if questioning reveals a prospect doing business in ways not compatible with righteousness, then we need to disengage or enlighten that prospect immediately (see Proverbs 13:20 and Ephesians 4:14).

Common Connections

We should question prospects in ways that find and build upon significant common connections.

Most of my customers throughout my professional career sold products or services to other people. In questioning prospects on how they sold, I often discovered prospects using unscrupulous schemes to get customers. Examples are a home-improvement company attempting to close sales without analyzing the needs of homeowners, and an automobile dealer being dishonest about the price of cars in their advertisements. In all instances of connecting with prospects whose belief system was not compatible with Christianity, the relationship ended poorly. I often felt cheated or frustrated because the prospect ended up treating me exactly like they treated their customers: with lies, deception, and things designed to serve their greed.

However, when I found prospects conducting business with integrity and righteously serving others, I became elated because I had a business partner and friend whose ways of conducting business were compatible with mine. We could connect in ways that motivated both of us to always do and say the righteous thing. Whatever was in the best interest of the other person became a priority, even if they had to say no to what I was selling, which allowed me to move on to better prospects. Occasionally, I had to refuse to let a prospect buy what I was selling, because I was certain it would not satisfy their needs or fulfill their expectations. Of course, this allowed the prospect to save their money for the things they truly needed.

Comfortable Chats

Throughout the Bible, I'm amazed at how comfortably God and people communicated. It shows us that when selling righteously, it's best to talk with people, not at them. We need to get their feedback and not say anything that would make the other person feel uncomfortable. This allows for conversations filled with truths and forthright opinions. We question prospects to uncover their needs because we want to deliver a solution that helps them overcome their challenges or present a solution that helps them make the best of their opportunities. So, we need prospects and customers who willingly and comfortably share sensitive information. As we arrive at solutions, everything discussed needs consideration, so we question thoroughly to gain a complete understanding of a prospect's buying process and needs. However, we don't need to discuss everything—only those things that righteously benefit the prospect as they relate to their business and any concerns that they mention (see Ephesians 4:29–31 and Ephesians 5:3–4).

We should focus and listen attentively without any preset agendas. We need to remain silent, not only refraining from speaking but also silencing the thoughts that travel through our minds as others speak. This allows us to listen righteously and comprehend superbly.

Prospects need an aura of comfort to share weighty information honestly. So, we speak in ways that construct comfort, not conflict. While selling, I try to avoid subjects such as politics or sex, any topic that may make a prospect feel uncomfortable. Before I worked in Christian radio, I also avoided discussing religion.

First Peter chapter 3 instructs us to search for peace and work to maintain it. So, we need to craft conversations in which information is shared, not argued about. For example, there are several marketing theories about what's needed for a successful advertising campaign. When I sold advertising, I could have argued for days about which theory should be applied to a particular situation. I tried to avoid these arguments by focusing conversations on things the prospect and I had in common. This meant I talked about the end results (campaign goals), which were generally generating revenue and or increasing store traffic. And I'd listen carefully to discover and address the prospect's personal challenges, as it related to achieving goals.

If I disagreed with a potential buyer about their marketing strategy, then I needed to honestly communicate that I could not recommend going forward with that proposed strategy. In some instances, I lost sales, but I gained favor because of my honesty. We must never sacrifice honesty for comfort.

Comforting Conversations

We must connect with people inside comfortable chats. Prospects need an aura of comfort to share sensitive information. So, we speak in ways that construct comfort, not conflict. We should also focus and listen attentively, without any preset agendas.

Care-filled Confrontations

At times, circumstances call for confrontations, as we seek to righteously resolve a problem or restore a relationship. In Genesis chapter 3, I noticed how God confronted Adam and Eve with questions after they had done something so grievous that it caused sin to enter the world.

Difficult issues need care-filled confrontations. So, we need to closely follow biblical principles. God instructs us in 1Peter chapter 3 to be tenderhearted, which means we should always be compassionate and gentle. He also instructs us to keep a humble attitude and not repay evil for evil.

We should lead with questions when a person needs to be confronted. Questions allow us to gain a better understanding and a proper perspective of any situation. They also allow us to understand the circumstances and empathize with the person during the confrontation. In our confrontations, we should follow the Bible, which states we should be quick to listen, slow to speak, and slow to become angry. Our anger will not cause others to behave righteously. After confronting the prospect with questions, we should avoid discussing things that may produce quarrels. As people selling righteously, we express ourselves in a kind manner that teaches and gently instructs. Hopefully, the person and issues being confronted are led to the truth. Our goal in confrontations is to uncover a truth that brings about a righteous resolution (see James 1:19–20 and 2 Timothy 2:23–26).

Resolve and Restore

Issues need to be carefully confronted in order to righteously resolve a problem or restore a relationship.

When I sold radio advertising, many of my prospects were professional buyers at advertising agencies. Sometimes, these buyers would put together advertising campaigns that included several radio stations, but not the station I represented. That aroused anger for several people at the radio station, including me, because it negatively impacted our incomes. The righteous thing for me to do in those situations was to confront the buyer with questions about why my station was not included.

My confrontation provided me with an opportunity to educate the buyer about the radio station, as well as an opportunity to build a righteous relationship. And, in several situations, my station was included the next time that buyer put together an advertising campaign, because of what the buyer learned about my radio station and the relationship cultivated during the confrontation. Also, what I learned in these confrontations armed me with strategies to sell other media buyers, who may have been considering excluding my radio station from a marketing plan, which included radio advertising. So, through care-filled confrontations, I became much better at preventing anyone from excluding a radio station that I represented.

Empathetic Evaluations

If prospects or customers are caught in challenging circumstances, we need to listen empathetically and be compassionate. This means we rid ourselves of any judgmental or condescending thoughts, as we seek to understand the emotional impact of their circumstances. God was very compassionate with Adam and Eve. As the Creator, He could have destroyed them both. We should learn from this example and use empathy and sympathy, as we question people. In 1 Peter chapter 3 and in several other places in the Bible, we are instructed to be sympathetic, and love each other as brothers and sisters.

With successful people, we need to rejoice with them even if their success eliminates their need for what we sell. I encountered several situations in which the prospects didn't need the type of advertising that I offered to continue being successful. With struggling customers and prospects, we need to offer them any free services that we have available and mourn with them about their situation. For example, with struggling clients, I would offer free consultations. I would also include them in promotions and charity initiatives that the radio station was doing, so that they could garner positive exposure. The Bible says that good will come to those who lend freely and conduct their affairs justly (see Psalm 112:5).

Love and Serve Righteously

We should be empathetic as we question prospects. People are living in all types of challenging circumstances. Our overall goal is to love and serve righteously.

Regardless of a prospect or customer's status, whether they're on the brink of bankruptcy or bathing in economic bliss, we don't always need to close a sale to build a righteous relationship. Our business goal is to build righteous relationships in which sales spring forth. Our life goal is to love and serve God and other people righteously. The Bible simply tells us to rejoice with those who are rejoicing and mourn with those who are mourning (see Romans 12:15, Zechariah 7:9, and 1 Peter 3:8–9).

Questions

1. What are the two best questions that you ask prospects?

2. How much time do you devote to developing and asking penetrating questions that help the prospect have a learning experience in which truth about their feelings and circumstances unfolds?

3. What type of "Assignments" do you develop during your consultations? Assignments are actions steps, with deadlines, which need to be completed by either or both the prospect and the salesperson.

4. When do you know that you've asked enough questions and gathered enough information to make a presentation?

5. What is your company's process for confronting dissatisfied or disruptive clients?

Scriptural References

- Consider God's first series of questions. We ask who, what, where, and when questions to verify the basic information about our prospect, which we gathered doing our research:

  But the LORD God called to the man, "Where are you?" He answered, "I heard you in the garden, and I was afraid because I was naked; so I hid." And he said, "Who told you that you were naked? Have you eaten from the tree that

I commanded you not to eat from?" The man said, "The woman you put here with me—she gave me some fruit from the tree, and I ate it." Then the LORD God said to the woman, "What is this you have done?" The woman said, "The serpent deceived me, and I ate" (Genesis 3:9–13).

- We should take action to seek the cooperation of others:

  Let us not become weary in doing good, for at the proper time we will reap a harvest if we do not give up. Therefore, as we have opportunity, let us do good to all people, especially to those who belong to the family of believers (Galatians 6:9–10).

  In the same way, faith by itself, if it is not accompanied by action, is dead (James 2:17).

- God's solution to Adam and Eve's sin problem included a vision of their future:

  So the LORD God said to the serpent, "Because you have done this, cursed are you above all the livestock and all the wild animals! You will crawl on your belly and you will eat dust all the days of your life. And I will put enmity between you and the woman, and between your offspring and hers; he will crush your head, and you will strike his heel."

  To the woman he said, "I will make your pains in childbearing very severe; with pain you will give birth to children. Your desire will be for your husband, and he will rule over you."

To Adam he said, "Because you listened to your wife and ate from the tree about which I commanded you, 'You must not eat of it,' cursed is the ground because of you; through painful toil you will eat food from it all the days of your life. It will produce thorns and thistles for you, and you will eat the plants of the field. By the sweat of your brow you will eat your food until you return to the ground, since from it you were taken; for dust you are and to dust you will return.' Adam named his wife Eve, because she would become the mother of all the living (Genesis 3:14–20).

- God gives us specific instructions for building and maintaining righteous relationships, regardless of circumstances:

  Finally, all of you, be like-minded, be sympathetic, love one another, be compassionate and humble. Do not repay evil with evil or insult with insult. On the contrary, repay evil with blessing, because to this you were called so that you may inherit a blessing. For, "Whoever would love life and see good days must keep their tongue from evil and their lips from deceitful speech. They must turn from evil and do good; they must seek peace and pursue it" (1 Peter 3:8–11).

- We treat people righteously regardless of how they treat us:

  "But to you who are listening I say: Love your enemies, do good to those who hate you, bless those who curse you, pray for those who mistreat you. If anyone slaps you on

one cheek, turn to them the other also. If someone takes your coat, do not withhold your shirt from them. Give to everyone who asks you, and if anyone takes what belongs to you, do not demand it back. Do to others as you would have them do to you" (Luke 6:27–31).

- We should question in ways that allow truth and transparency to flourish:

  He said to them, "Do you bring in a lamp to put it under a bowl or a bed? Instead, don't you put it on its stand? For whatever is hidden is meant to be disclosed, and whatever is concealed is meant to be brought out into the open (Mark 4:21–22).

  Therefore, each of you must put off falsehood and speak truthfully to his neighbor, for we are members of one body (Ephesians 4:25).

- We should question prospects in ways that build significant, compatible connections, discussing principles and beliefs behind answers:

  Walk with the wise and become wise, for a companion of fools suffers harm (Proverbs 13:20).

  Then we will no longer be infants, tossed back and forth by the waves, and blown here and there by every wind of teaching and by the cunning and craftiness of people in their deceitful scheming (Ephesians 4:14).

- We must connect with prospects in comfortable chats, discussing only those things that are helpful in building relationships and meeting needs:

  Do not let any unwholesome talk come out of your mouths, but only what is helpful for building others up according to their needs, that it may benefit those who listen. And do not grieve the Holy Spirit of God, with whom you were sealed for the day of redemption. Get rid of all bitterness, rage and anger, brawling and slander, along with every form of malice (Ephesians 4:29–31).

  But among you there must not be even a hint of sexual immorality, or of any kind of impurity, or of greed, because these are improper for God's holy people. Nor should there be obscenity, foolish talk or coarse joking, which are out of place, but rather thanksgiving (Ephesians 5:3–4).

- We need to handle confrontations carefully, being quick to listen, slow to speak, and slow to become angry:

  My dear brothers, take note of this: Everyone should be quick to listen, slow to speak and slow to become angry, because human anger does not produce the righteousness that God desires (James 1:19–20).

  Don't have anything to do with foolish and stupid arguments, because you know they produce quarrels. And the Lord's servant must not be quarrelsome but must be kind to everyone, able to teach, not resentful. Opponents must be gently instructed, in the hope that God will grant them repentance leading to a knowledge of the truth, and that they will come to their senses and escape from the trap of the devil, who has taken them captive to do his will (2 Timothy 2:23–26).

- When working with struggling customers and prospects, we should offer any free services that are available. The Bible says that good will come to those who lend freely and conduct their affairs justly:

  Good will come to those who are generous and lend freely, who conduct their affairs with justice (Psalm 112:5).

- With successful people, we need to rejoice with them even if their success eliminates their need for what we sell:

  Rejoice with those who rejoice; mourn with those who mourn (Romans 12:15).

- We must be compassionate, sympathizing and empathizing with everyone:

  "This is what the Lord Almighty says: 'Administer true justice; show mercy and compassion to one another'" (Zechariah 7:9).

  Finally, all of you, be like-minded, be sympathetic, love one another, be compassionate and humble" (1 Peter 3:8).

CHAPTER 7:

Presentations

Follow God's example, therefore, as dearly loved children and walk in the way of love, just as Christ loved us and gave himself up for us as a fragrant offering and sacrifice to God. But among you there must not be even a hint of sexual immorality, or of any kind of impurity, or of greed, because these are improper for God's holy people. Nor should there be obscenity, foolish talk or coarse joking, which are out of place, but rather thanksgiving. For of this you can be sure: No immoral, impure or greedy person—such a man is an idolater—has any inheritance in the Kingdom of Christ and of God. Let no one deceive you with empty words, for because of such things God's wrath comes on those who are disobedient. Therefore do not be partners with them. For you were once darkness, but now you are light in the Lord. Live as children of light (for the fruit of the light consists in all goodness, righteousness, and truth) and find out what pleases the Lord.

—Ephesians 5:1–10

Children of Light

In AD 60, the Apostle Paul sent a letter to the Christians in Ephesus explaining how to continue living righteously. He presented several principles that we must incorporate to continue selling God's way. At this point in the sales process, a prospect has approached us needing specific information, or we've found a prospect and gathered enough information to make a presentation. Nevertheless, a presentation is needed. The presentation is an opportunity to shine a light on what we sell at a time when the prospect's level of attentiveness is high.

The first thing Paul says in Ephesians chapter 5 is that we need to be imitators of God. To help us reach that goal, I'll examine two biblical presentations, one by God the Father and the other by Jesus. Both help as we strive to be imitators of God during our presentations (see Ephesians 5:1).

When God appears to Moses at the burning bush and when Jesus washes His disciples' feet at the Last Supper, we find the three components that are needed for any sales presentation. First, the presentations arise out of previously gathered information; second, they offer a way to solve problems or maximize opportunities; third, they include a vision of the future with the proposed solution in place. The presentation to Moses serves as an example of how to present to one decision-maker. The presentation to Jesus's disciples gives us an example of how to present to multiple decision-makers. In the presentation to Moses, God offers a tangible solution in leading the Israelites out of Egypt. At the Last Supper, Jesus offers more of an intangible solution in His promise of blessings for the disciples. Selling God's way prepares us to make presentations, regardless of the number of decision-makers or the complexity of what we sell.

Three Basic Components of a Sales Presentation

1. The presentation arises out of previously gathered information.
2. The presentation offers a way to solve problems or maximize opportunities.
3. The presentation includes a vision of the future.

The Burning Bush Presentation: God Speaks to Moses

There the angel of the LORD appeared to him in flames of fire from within a bush. Moses saw that though the bush was on fire it did not burn up. So Moses thought, "I will go over and see this strange sight—why the bush does not burn up."

When the LORD saw that he had gone over to look, God called to him from within the bush, "Moses! Moses!" And Moses said, "Here I am." "Do not come any closer," God said. "Take off your sandals, for the place where you are standing is holy ground." Then he said, "I am the God of your father, the God of Abraham, the God of Isaac and the God of Jacob." At this, Moses hid his face, because he was afraid to look at God.

The LORD said, "I have indeed seen the misery of my people in Egypt. I have heard them crying out because of their slave drivers, and I am concerned about their suffering. So I have come down to rescue them from the hand of the Egyptians and to bring them up out of that land into a good and spacious land, a land flowing with

> *milk and honey—the home of the Canaanites, Hittites, Amorites, Perizzites, Hivites, and Jebusites. And now the cry of the Israelites has reached me, and I have seen the way the Egyptians are oppressing them. So now, go. I am sending you to Pharaoh to bring my people the Israelites out of Egypt."*
>
> *But Moses said to God, "Who am I, that I should go to Pharaoh and bring the Israelites out of Egypt?" And God said, "I will be with you. And this will be the sign to you that it is I who have sent you: When you have brought the people out of Egypt, you will worship God on this mountain."*
>
> —Exodus 3:2–12

For our purposes, I'll examine this interaction in the context of the three basic components needed for any sales presentation. In verse 7, the Lord says, "*I have indeed seen the misery of my people in Egypt. I have heard them crying out because of their slave drivers, and I am concerned about their suffering.*" This represents the previously gathered information that gave birth to the presentation. Our presentations must arise out of verifiable information. God confirmed verifiable information to Moses before He presented the solution to Moses.

In verse 8, God says, "*So I have come down to rescue them from the hand of the Egyptians, and to bring them up out of that land into a good and spacious land, a land flowing with milk and honey—the home of the Canaanites, Hittites, Amorites, Perizzites, Hivites, and Jebusites.*" This represents the solution to the problem of the Israelites being enslaved. The solution in our presentation must provide specifics regarding what we intend to do and how we plan on doing it. God explained what He intended to do and how He was going to do it in His presentation to Moses.

In verse 12, the Lord says, "*I will be with you. And this will be the sign to you that it is I who have sent you: when you have brought the people out of Egypt, you will worship God on this mountain.*" This represents the vision of the future with the solution in place. Our presentations must include a description of the future with the solution in place. God gave Moses a vision, an idea, of what the future will be like after the solution is in place.

Seven Elements We Can Imitate

1. *The Presentation Takes Place on Holy Ground.* Where we present impacts the quality of the entire presentation; any place that accentuates our capabilities and resources can serve as our "sacred" selling ground. This could be our office, a conference room, or the prospect's location. Face-to-face presentations in these places illuminate what we offer, while reinforcing the credibility of what we communicate.

Sacred Selling Ground

Where we give our presentation impacts its overall quality; any place that accentuates our capabilities and resources can serve as our "sacred" selling ground. Presentations in these places should illuminate what we offer, while reinforcing the credibility of what we communicate.

In selling advertising, having prospects at the radio station viewing the oversized call letters, meeting the on-air personalities, and hearing the station blasted throughout the hallways always served as the best environment for delivering a presentation. In selling eggs, my grandfather and I would often bring the eggs to someone's kitchen. Being in the prospect's kitchen with a dozen eggs made it easy for them to buy eggs and place them in their refrigerator.

2. *A Burning Bush Serves to Get Attention.* When we begin a presentation, it's important to grab a prospect's undivided attention. Using simple objects as tools for communicating helps to get prospects to focus on what we present. Thought-provoking revelations or penetrating questions can also serve as attention-grabbing tools. Beginning a presentation this way provides us an opportunity to attract attention and gather momentum to clear the prospect's mind of distractions, which contributes to the prospect's focus and comprehension.

   In selling books door-to-door, it was important to start presentations by opening a book and showing a powerful photo. This focused the prospect's attention on the photo and created interest in the book. Likewise, in selling advertising, opening a presentation with a radio commercial that featured the prospect's business immediately ignited their interest. These commercials demonstrated the persuasive power of radio and created an ideal environment for selling more radio advertising time.

3. *God Identifies Himself.* In the burning bush presentation, God tells Moses that He is the God of his father and of Abraham, Isaac, and Jacob. After God identifies Himself, Moses hides his face out of reverent fear. Before we get into the specifics of what we offer, a prospect needs to understand who we are, and what we can do. We need to identify ourselves through our capabilities and resources. We do this by presenting evidence that demonstrates what our company has accomplished and what we're capable of achieving. This takes the prospect beyond any superficial awareness of who we represent and what we sell.

   Presenting a company mission statement isn't enough. We need to present evidence that proves these statements exist as more than just words. This evidence needs to be visible and verifiable. Client testimonials and referrals help greatly in this area. Supportive statements from clients can be very powerful; including them in presentations with as much detail as possible helps in establishing our company's capabilities. It sends a strong message that our company can fulfill expectations and deliver the promised results.

   While selling books, I always used the names of my prospect's neighbors who bought from me, to help a prospect understand my validity and value. While selling advertising, I used the names and experiences of satisfied clients, to validate my radio station's services.

   Also, prospects perceive products and services through the person doing the selling. This makes the salesperson part of the product and service. So, our individual capabilities and resources need to be included in the presentations. This is especially effective in competitive selling arenas. As people selling God's way, we need to highlight our education, individual client successes, and commitment to righteousness. We should discuss our problem-solving skills, professional contacts, and ability to do things correctly the first time. All this helps in getting a prospect to fully understand the value associated with what we sell.

4. *The Presentation Features a Description of the Problem or Opportunity.* In the burning bush presentation, God twice mentions the Israelites' plight in Egypt. Moses accepts God's solution soon after the presentation, choosing not to ponder the decision for days or weeks. Prospects will buy more quickly if they believe we understand their problems completely. Featuring the problem or opportunity in the presentation helps to reinforce the importance of our solution. It also creates a sense of urgency for putting it in place. Ideally, soon after the presentation, the prospect will agree to buy.

Problems and Opportunities

Featuring the problem or opportunity in the presentation helps to reinforce the importance of our solution. It also creates a sense of urgency for putting it in place.

In reviewing my sales results, I discovered that whenever I struggled to articulate a problem or opportunity, while preparing a presentation, the entire presentation invariably suffered, because it lacked detail in exactly how to solve the problem or take advantage of the opportunity. This always led to a quick rejection (no sale) or an extended process in which it took an inordinate amount of time to close a sale. I learned to prevent these scenarios by pausing whenever struggling to clearly conceptualize a prospect's problem or opportunity. I would review the entire sales process for thoroughness and righteousness, I would ask myself several questions:

- Did I question thoroughly enough to uncover true needs?
- Do I possess sufficient insights as to the origins of the problem or opportunity?
- Did I hear the prospect express fears, frustrations, or dissatisfaction when discussing the problem?
- Did I hear the prospect express desire, excitement, or eagerness when discussing the opportunity?
- Do I need to question other decision-makers?

Sometimes, I would still struggle to fully understand the prospect's problem or opportunity even after I had analyzed the sales process. In such cases, I would conclude that I needed to restart the entire sales process by analyzing the prospect in comparison to my angelic customer profile. Then I would quickly contact the decision-maker(s) to ask additional questions for discovery purposes and clarification. If I discovered in my examination that I had gone through the sales process correctly, but still struggled to articulate the problem or opportunity, I would move on to other prospects because what I was selling was not needed. If I discovered that I had questioned incorrectly the first time, but a new problem or opportunity existed, then I would develop a presentation based on the most recent information.

5. *God Gives Moses Specific Instructions.* Prospects need to know exactly what they need to do to complete the sales transaction. Including this information in the presentation shows our commitment to honesty, while giving the prospect an opportunity to raise objections. This sets the stage for closing the sale. It also avoids putting prospects in a position where they're confronted with unexpected terms or conditions after they agreed to buy, or as they ponder their decision to buy. Generally speaking, no one likes surprises, and everyone appreciates honesty.

   One of the worst feelings I know is going back to a prospect after a presentation with more conditions they must complete to finalize the sale. This always opens the door to distrust. The prospect might believe I had intentionally withheld the information to make a quick sale or that I was unaware of important information because of incompetence. Either scenario raises a red flag of doubt or distrust, potentially damaging the perception of my credibility and capabilities. Whenever I needed to deliver potentially bad news after a presentation, I tried to compensate the client by giving them something of value along with the unpleasant information. In book sales, this might be a free set of books; in advertising sales, this might be a free week of commercials. Such compensation allowed me to accept responsibility for the mistake and present something that demonstrated my capabilities and my commitment to righteousness.

6. *Moses Questions God.* Questions from the prospect need to be part of any sales presentation. During the presentation, we need the prospect's attention, interest, and participation. We can assess to what degree we have these things if the prospect asks questions. The depth of the questions asked exposes the prospect's level of interest. Questions that require in-depth answers reflect a high level of interest, because they call for education or clarification, allowing us to present even more of what we sell.

   Moses asks God an in-depth question that God could have taken a whole chapter to explain. He asks God, "*Who am I, that I should go to Pharaoh and bring the Israelites out of Egypt*?" Moses's question leads God to present the details about how the Israelites were going to be brought out of Egypt. And it answered Moses's question about who he was and detailed his God-given assignment.

   In reading Exodus chapter 3 and the first sixteen verses of Exodus chapter 4, we see that Moses is keenly interested in how to accomplish what God presented. So, he asks God even more questions about how to lead the Israelites out of Egypt. A series of questions asked during a presentation indicate a high level of interest, as they call for salespeople to present more information and benefits. We need to hear questions during our presentations that require us to explain how, and why, our solution or opportunity works.

At the end of this story, Moses's final comment to God is, "*Pardon your servant, Lord. Please send someone else*" (Exodus 4:13). Although Moses is keenly interested in the Israelites escaping Egypt, he does not buy into the solution being presented. Of course, God overcomes Moses's objection and secures his commitment to lead the Israelites out of captivity.

If a prospect did not ask questions during one of my presentations, I would stop near the halfway point. Then I asked the prospect questions that assessed their level of attentiveness and interest. I'd ask for their thoughts, good or bad, about what I am presenting. I'd ask if they wanted me to continue the presentation or come back at another time. I might ask whether what I am selling is something they might buy. Depending on their answer, my next step would be to continue the presentation (if I found the prospect attuned and leaning toward buying) or stop the presentation and go back through the questioning stage of the sales process, searching for more substantive needs.

7. *God Gives Moses a Guarantee.* God gives Moses the guarantee that He will be with him always. God's guarantee allows Moses to buy into leading the Israelites, knowing that regardless of what happens, he will always have with

him the Creator of the universe, who possesses infinite wisdom and power. In our presentations, we need to hand out as many guarantees as possible. Our guarantees should arise out of truths rooted in reliable research, empirical evidence, or trusted testimonies. These guarantees provide justification for buying what we sell. It permits prospects to purchase what we sell, knowing that they'll own what's guaranteed, regardless of what else happens. However, we must exercise caution about presenting guarantees. Overpromising or guaranteeing something that has the slightest probability of not happening is unacceptable for people selling righteously.

Guarantee It

In our presentations, we need to hand out as many guarantees as possible.

I was always extremely cautious in handing out guarantees, especially when I sold advertising, because it is impossible to predict the exact number of sales or inquiries that occur following a radio commercial. Even though past campaigns may have yielded a specific number of sales and inquiries, a future campaign could yield different results. A competitor pricing more aggressively, a technological change that decreases demand for what's being advertised, or adverse weather conditions making it difficult for customers to drive to a retail outlet are examples of the unpredictable things that can affect the results of an ad campaign. Also, a significant part of what happens during an ad campaign remains too complicated for accurate measurements. For example, the number of people moving from unawareness to awareness or moving from awareness to interest can significantly impact the results.

In selling advertising, I discussed all that could occur in an ad campaign. However, I only guaranteed those elements we could be sure of based on reliable research and empirical evidence. For instance, research revealed statistics such as audience size, percentage of homeowners, or percentage of car buyers. Empirical evidence allowed me to make guarantees about verifiable things, such as the radio station's format or the geographical area where their advertising message would be heard. When I sold tangible products such as eggs and books, the guarantees were easier to present because a potential buyer could see and touch the product and take immediate delivery of what I was guaranteeing.

The Last Supper Presentation: Jesus Washes His Disciples' Feet

The second biblical presentation that we will study is Jesus with His disciples at the Last Supper. Once again, for our purposes, I'll examine this event in the context of the three basic components of any sales presentation:

- Arises out of previously gathered information.
- Offers a way to solve problems or maximize opportunities.
- Includes a vision of the future.

It was just before the Passover Feast. Jesus knew that the time had come for him to leave this world and go to the Father. Having loved his own who were in the world, He now showed them the full extent of his love.

The evening meal was being served, and the devil had already prompted Judas Iscariot, son of Simon, to betray Jesus. Jesus knew that the Father had put all things under his power, and that he had come from God and was returning to God; so he got up from the meal, took off his outer clothing, and wrapped a towel around his waist. After that, he poured water into a basin and began to wash his disciples' feet, drying them with the towel that was wrapped around him.

He came to Simon Peter, who said to him, "Lord, are you going to wash my feet?" Jesus replied, "You do not realize now what I am doing, but later you will understand." "No," said Peter, "you shall never wash my feet." Jesus answered, "Unless I wash you, you have no part with me." "Then, Lord," Simon Peter replied, "not just my feet but my hands and my head as well!" Jesus answered, "A person who has had a bath needs only to wash his feet; his whole body is clean. And you are clean, though not every one of you." For he knew who was going to betray him, and that was why he said not everyone was clean.

When he had finished washing their feet, he put on his clothes and returned to his place. "Do you understand what I have done for you?" he asked them. "You call me 'Teacher' and 'Lord,' and rightly so, for that is what I

> *am. Now that I, your Lord and Teacher, have washed your feet, you also should wash one another's feet. I have set you an example that you should do as I have done for you. Very truly, I tell you, no servant is greater than his master, nor is a messenger greater than the one who sent him. Now that you know these things, you will be blessed if you do them."*
>
> —John 13:1–17

In John chapter 13, verses 1 through 3 represent the previously known information that gave birth to the presentation, the first component needed for any sales presentation. Jesus knows He is going to betrayed and crucified. In this presentation, He prepares the disciples for events that will change their lives forever.

In verses 12 through 15, Jesus offers the disciples a way to maximize an opportunity, which is the second component needed in sales presentations. He says, "*Do you understand what I have done for you? . . . You call me 'Teacher' and 'Lord,' and rightly so, for that is what I am. Now that I, your Lord and Teacher, have washed your feet, you also should wash one another's feet. I have set you an example that you should do as I have done for you.*" In these verses, Jesus gives the disciples a solution to humankind's sin problem. His example of washing the disciples' feet gives them a way to behave to maximize their opportunity to save souls. Jesus does not want them to wash feet simply as a way of being nice to each other. By humbling Himself and serving, Jesus demonstrates how they can serve anyone after He is gone. They can lead others to Jesus who washes away sins and offers an eternal life in Heaven after death.

In verse 17, Jesus says, "*Now that you know these things, you will be blessed, if you do them.*" This verse represents the vision of the future, which is the third component needed in any sales presentation. If the disciples humble themselves and serve in a way that lead others to follow Jesus Christ, who washes away sins and offers eternal life in paradise, then they too will be blessed, taking advantage of the opportunity presented to them.

Three Things to Imitate when Presenting to Multiple Decision-Makers

- *Build a Relationship with Each Decision-Maker.* Our presentations must address the concerns of each decision-maker. Previously, I discussed the importance of uncovering and questioning anyone who influences the buying decision. In this stage, we build upon what we have learned to present a solution or opportunity for everyone, who can say yes or no to buying what we sell. Jesus took the time to wash all twelve disciples' feet, including those of Judas, even though Jesus knew that Judas was the disciple who would betray Him. In washing each disciple's feet, Jesus showed His desire to serve each person, regardless of their sin and any unrighteousness. Next, He built upon the relationship with each disciple by offering each one the opportunity to do as He had done. The disciples who took advantage of this opportunity guaranteed themselves a blessing.

  Once I began conducting business-to-business sales transactions (selling advertising), most of my sales involved multiple decision-makers. Typically, three or more people representing three different concerns:

- A professional buyer concerned with the technical aspects of what I sold.
- An executive buyer whose concerns centered on my product's ability to deliver the features and benefits that were presented.
- A client buyer concerned about the economic impact of buying what I sold—the cost and return on that investment.

I often started the sales process with the most accessible buyer, usually the professional buyer. In selling advertising, this person was often called the media buyer. In the questioning stage, I would consult with the media buyer to uncover information about the other decision-makers to gain greater insights into the organization's decision-making process. I would also question people outside the media department and business associates who may have conducted business with my prospect. I did this because at times professionals outside the media department and business associates were willing to share more information about the prospect's priorities and processes than the media buyer.

My goal was to establish a righteous relationship with everyone, while uncovering the roles and responsibilities of each decision-maker. If I was unable to directly communicate with a decision-maker, then I relied on my customer knowledge and the information gathered through others to deliver a presentation that met the needs of each decision-maker, even if I never directly met that person.

- *Devote More Time to Key People.* Much of your time should be devoted to the most influential people in your prospect's buying process. In the previous stages, we discovered the roles and responsibilities of each decision-maker. In this stage, we spend significant time with the most influential person.

In the presentation above, only two disciples get mentioned by name: Peter and Judas. Other disciples are mentioned in the discussion after the washing of the feet is completed, in a sort of question-and-answer session. But Peter and Judas are mentioned during the washing of the disciples' feet. They are arguably the two most influential disciples. Both have significant roles in leading millions to God through Jesus Christ. The only disciple Jesus converses with during the presentation is Peter. Jesus had declared beforehand that the church will be built upon Peter's revelation that Jesus is the Messiah, the Christ and Son of the living God. Jesus also knows that Judas's betrayal will lead to His death and resurrection. Jesus's death followed by His resurrection is the final proof that He is, who He says He is, Lord and Savior for everyone (see Matthew 16:13–17 and John 12: 44–47).

When I sold advertising, there could be as many as six people who could say yes or no to buying what I was selling. To ascertain which individual held the most influence, I needed to understand the prospect's buying process. This meant I spent significant time in the questioning stage uncovering the prospect's personnel, priorities, and procedures. Once I discovered the names and titles of the key decision-makers, I spent most of my time communicating with them. Sometimes, because of a prospect's buying process, I was unable to work directly with a key decision-maker. In those situations, I still focused my presentation on addressing the concerns of the most influential decision-makers.

- *Prepare Each Prospect to Sell.* Getting a commitment from each disciple to follow Him was one of the first things Jesus did at the start of His earthly ministry. Jesus prepared them to undertake the mission of leading others to God. The Gospels are filled with examples of Jesus presenting the facts and benefits of His ministry with His disciples present. He also prepares them to handle any objections to His ministry. In the Last Supper presentation, He shows the disciples how to persuade and lead as He had.

Three Things We Must Do to Prepare Each Prospect to Sell

It's highly unlikely that all the decision-makers will be at the sales presentations. What typically occurs is that the decision-makers at the presentation pass along the information to those who are absent. To overcome this selling handicap, we need to go through the following three steps to prepare each person at our presentation to sell, as they pass along our information to other decision-makers.

- *Secure a buying commitment from each prospect at the presentation, that's in alignment with their role and area of responsibility.* So, we should ask prospects their opinion of what we just presented. Then ask or confirm that they will be positively recommending or submitting our product through their buying process. This must be done as quickly as possible, because "should we buy?" Discussions between decision-makers often take place right after presentations. Securing any buying commitment from a decision-maker at the presentation allows us to transition into discussions about decision-makers not at our presentation. Chapter 8 covers closing sales and securing buying commitments.
- *Discuss any possible objection that a decision-maker not at the presentation may have.* We must ask those at our presentations if they know of or can anticipate any objection that an absent decision-maker may express. Chapter 9 deals with handling objections.
- *Rehearse with each prospect what to say and show, as they pass along our information.* When I sold advertising, I made it a priority to rehearse with prospects what to say as they passed along my information. I would say things like "Please show this research piece" or "Please don't start your conversation by saying that you're recommending buying radio ads. Please start by saying that you've found a solution to the decline in weekend website traffic." I needed prospects presenting my product in the same context I had just presented it to them—as an offer to solve a problem or maximize an opportunity, not as an offer to spend money on a product or service.

In one of the final verses of the Last Supper presentation, Jesus tells His disciples that they should do for each other just as He has done for them. That's essentially what we're asking of each decision-maker at our presentation: to present our information to any decision-maker, not at the presentation, as we presented it to them.

In conclusion, if we're selling in any scenario that involves multiple decision-makers, we should add the following three elements from Jesus's Last Supper presentation to the seven characteristics from Moses's burning bush presentation:

- We need to build a personal relationship with all accessible decision-makers.
- We should devote most of our time and attention to persuading the key decision-makers who exert the most influence, even if they're not accessible and no personal relationship exists.
- We must prepare each accessible decision-maker to present our information to any absent decision-maker.

What We Can and Cannot Imitate

Obviously, there are aspects of godly presentations that we cannot imitate, such as walking on water, parting the seas, or raising people from the dead. However, we should create presentations that amaze and awe by using boldness, parables, confidence, service, visions, instructions, and technical enhancements that add value to audio or video elements.

Only God is all-powerful and all-wise, able to completely solve all problems, and provide endless opportunities. So, as people selling righteously, we need to realize the limits of what we can present. For example, when selling eggs, I could not say that buying my eggs would solve a hunger problem or enable a person to create fabulous food dishes. Buying eggs only solved part of the hunger problem or provided only one ingredient for making a meal. In selling advertising, I could not say that buying radio advertising would completely solve a marketing problem or completely maximize a sales opportunity. Buying the advertising was just a necessary step in solving the marketing problem or maximizing the selling opportunity. In each client's situation, many other components are needed before a problem can be completely solved, or an opportunity totally maximized.

For example, a technology company could purchase radio advertising to market its amazing new software. However, if they don't have proper pricing, competent sellers, and adequate distribution, their advertising cannot singlehandedly enable them to maximize the opportunity made possible by their sensational new product.

Paul's Advice

In Ephesian chapter 5, Paul tells all believers that in everything we do, there must not be a hint of sexual immorality or any kind of impurity or greed because these things are improper for God's holy people. He also says that there should not be any obscenity, foolish talk, or coarse joking. These instructions also apply as we deliver presentations. Bringing such things into our work ignores God's instructions and invites Satan into our sales process. Jesus says in John 10:10 that Satan comes to kill, steal, and destroy.

Paul also says that we are not to let anyone deceive us with empty words and that we should not partner with such people. He is not telling us not to associate with sinners; he is warning us not to be deceived by them, allowing ourselves to fall into sin. The temptation to sin often arrives through the advice of others. As salespeople, we get advice from managers, mentors, and friends about what to say or do while selling. If this advice calls for deception (inaccurate research), greed (overstated benefits), or slander (maligning the competition), we must discard it because Scripture forbids this type of behavior (see Ephesians 5:3–4 and John 10:10).

As people selling God's way, our presentations should include content that is rooted in righteousness such as like fair pricing and honest estimations. We should embrace Paul's advice and behave as children of the light. The fruit of this light consists of truth and conduct that please God. Our presentations should include the truth, and they should be filled with workable solutions, viable opportunities, and service-minded goals.

Questions

1. Do you include guarantees in your presentations? If no, why not? If yes, what kinds of guarantees do you make?

2. Do you include questions as an integral part of your presentations?

3. How do you build relationships with each decision-maker in selling scenarios that come with multiple decision-makers? Do you prepare prospects to sell to other prospects?

4. What do you think Jesus would say about your sales presentations?

Scriptural References

1. We must be followers of Jesus in all that we do, which obviously includes all aspects of our selling behavior:

   "Follow God's example, therefore, as dearly loved children" (Ephesians 5:1).

2. We should confirm our identity and purpose as it relates to what we are selling whenever the opportunity arises. Jesus confirmed His identity and mission to His disciples several times throughout the Scripture:

   When Jesus came to the region of Caesarea Philippi, he asked his disciples, "Who do people say the Son of Man is?" They replied, "Some say John the Baptist; others say Elijah; and still others, Jeremiah or one of the prophets." "But what about you?" he asked. "Who do you say I am?" Simon Peter answered, "You are the Messiah, the Son of the living God." Jesus replied, "Blessed are you, Simon son of Jonah, for this was not revealed to you by flesh and blood, but by my Father in heaven" (Matthew 16:13–17).

Then Jesus cried out, "Whoever believes in me does not believe in me only, but in the one who sent me. The one who looks at me is seeing the one who sent me. I have come into the world as a light, so that no one who believes in me should stay in darkness. If anyone hears my words but does not keep them, I do not judge that person. For I did not come to judge the world, but to save the world" (John 12:44–47).

3. Our sales presentation should be void of offensive language and anything that could be construed as unrighteous or sinful, inviting evil or even Satan into our sales process. Our presentations are rooted in righteousness and Christ-centered living.

   But among you there must not be even a hint of sexual immorality, or of any kind of impurity, or of greed, because these are improper for God's holy people. Nor should there be obscenity, foolish talk or coarse joking, which are out of place, but rather thanksgiving (Ephesians 5:3–4).

   The thief comes only to steal and kill and destroy; I have come that they may have life, and have it to the full (John 10:10).

CHAPTER 8:

Closing

Then the eleven disciples went to Galilee, to the mountain where Jesus had told them to go. When they saw him, they worshiped him; but some doubted. Then Jesus came to them and said, "All authority in Heaven and on earth has been given to me. Therefore go and make disciples of all nations, baptizing them in the name of the Father and of the Son and of the Holy Spirit, and teaching them to obey everything I have commanded you. And surely I am with you always, to the very end of the age."

—Matthew 28:16–20

The Great Commission

According to the Gospel of Matthew, Jesus makes the above statements to His disciples atop a mountain before ascending into heaven. While some of the disciples are on this mountain worshiping Jesus, others are there harboring doubts. It's hard to believe anyone who has witnessed Jesus's miracles, death, and resurrection would hold any doubts about following Him. In the Gospel of John, Jesus commends those who have not witnessed yet are faithful followers with no doubts (see John 20:29).

In the Great Commission, Jesus urges His disciples to commit, to go, and make disciples. He states in verses 19 and 20, "*Therefore go . . . surely I am with you always, to the very end of the age.*" Because Jesus was gloriously effective in His ministry, millions (including these disciples) follow Him forever. For our purposes, these closing statements serve as an example of how we should close a sale. Closing is the essence of a salesperson's job. If we can't close, we can't sell. Closing involves completing the necessary steps to secure the prospect's commitment to buy. Our closing actions should spur the final buying reactions, which then get transformed into an agreement, contract, or payment.

The Job

Closing is the essence of a salesperson's job. If we can't close, we can't sell.

Natural or Logical Conclusion

Throughout Jesus's earthly ministry, He led the disciples to make commitments. First, the disciples committed to leave their homes and follow Him. Then they committed themselves to His teachings, and finally, the disciples committed to making more disciples. After witnessing Jesus's death and resurrection, it would seem natural to continue following His instructions. Yet from the opening verse in this passage, we see that some of the disciples still had doubts, when Jesus commanded them to go and make disciples.

This process of getting minor commitments before securing a major commitment is a key component of selling successfully. Minor commitments require prospects to participate in the sale process by giving us their time, attention, and cooperation before they give us any money. Throughout our sales process, we should be continually getting prospects to make minor commitments. The first commitment usually involves agreeing to a meeting. The next commitments involve answering questions and giving their undivided attention to our presentation. Thereafter, the commitments center on buying what we present. Attaining the major commitment, where the prospects buy what we are selling, is the next logical step. But it's *our* responsibility as salespeople to secure this commitment, even when a prospect holds doubts about buying what we sell.

There are various ways to ask prospects to buy or to get them to commit to buying. Most often, closing works best when it involves a prospect following instructions. We can begin closing anytime during the presentation. However, it's best to close immediately after a presentation. In situations with more than one decision-maker, we can close all the decision-makers at the same time, by constructing a group close that addresses the concerns of each buyer. We can also approach each decision-maker after the presentation with the intent of closing the sale.

Any decent salesperson's character must contain a closing conscience that drives them to deliver those closing words, be they statements, instructions, or questions. While it's best to close face-to-face, closing via a phone call, letter, or email is acceptable. A prospect agreeing to buy before we close only indicates that we could have begun closing sooner.

For people selling God's way, successful closing always includes three parts: a principle, a program, and a promise. How we shape and deliver the closing principle, program, and promise depends on who we sell to and their buying process. However, regardless of who we sell to, the closing principle, program, and promise must be communicated with confidence and specificity. After our close, the prospect should clearly see that buying from us is smart and satisfying.

Close Righteously

There are various ways to ask a prospect to buy or to get them to commit to buying. Most often, closing works best when it involves a prospect following instructions. For people selling God's way, successful closing always includes three parts: a principle, a program, and a promise.

Principle, Program, Promise

The closing principle summarizes the perspective the prospect should hold about what we sell. This principle arises out of a truth that we undoubtedly believe about the features and benefits of what we are selling. The closing principle justifies the closing program.

The closing program instructs the prospect as to what to do, or affirms what the prospect will do to buy what we are selling. The closing program should also be clearly understood and spark a sense of urgency. The program, if followed, should facilitate closing a sale as succinctly and as swiftly as possible.

The closing promise predicts the outcome if the prospect adheres to the principle and follows the program. The promise may predict something that's tangible or intangible. However, it must be logical and practical, something that the prospect views as vital to solving a problem or maximizing an opportunity.

Here are some examples. I'm using the first example only in the context of how we should close sales. Obviously, these Scriptures hold a much higher significance.

Closing Example: Jesus, in the Final Chapter of Matthew

Principle: "*Then Jesus came to them and said, 'All authority in Heaven and on earth has been given to me*'" (Matthew 28:18). This is the closing principle that the disciples should embrace as truth—that all authority in Heaven and on earth had been given to Jesus. Through His virgin birth, death, and resurrection, along with countless other miracles, Jesus had established this principle to be true. Therefore, the disciples should willingly follow the instructions of their Lord and Savior, Jesus Christ, and follow the program that He outlines.

Program: "*Therefore go and make disciples of all nations, baptizing them in the name of the Father and of the Son and of the Holy Spirit. And teaching them to obey everything I have commanded you*" (Matthew 28:19–20). These specific instructions were to be completed by the disciples because of the closing principle, which confirmed that Jesus had all authority to command and control any circumstances or anything.

Promise: "*And surely I am with you always, to the very end of the age*" (Matthew 28:20). This promise will be fulfilled if the disciples follow the closing program, which is the instruction Jesus gave the disciples to go and make more disciples. This promise empowers the disciples to travel throughout the world and make other disciples, knowing that Jesus who holds all authority, is their ally and is with them always. This same Jesus who did numerous miracles and even conquered death to rise and live again, after being crucified, has just promised each disciple eternal love and companionship.

Closing Example: My Grandfather Selling Eggs in 1965

Principle: "These eggs are fresh. They're laid locally, and I sell them for less than those at the grocery store." My grandfather's belief was based on the fact that he kept the hens that laid the eggs. Afterward, he would review the prices at the grocery store before setting his price. Because this is the truth, his closing principle, that he wanted his potential buyers to accept to follow his program, which were his instructions for buying the eggs.

Program: "Give me 35 cents, and I'll give you eggs you can use for cooking all types of dishes." Prospects needed to follow these simple instructions to receive the eggs. My grandfather's closing program, if followed, facilitated closing a sale quickly.

Promise: "When you use these eggs, you'll see that they are just as good as, or better than, those at a grocery store. Plus, they cost less." This logical and practical promise will be fulfilled if the prospect follows the program and uses the eggs for preparing meals. My grandfather's closing promise is ideal because it predicts the future, if the prospect adheres to the principle and follows the program.

Closing Example: Me Selling Advertising in 2005

Principle: "My radio station delivers the audience needed for accomplishing your marketing goals." This is a truth I communicated after much research and several discussions with the prospect to verify their target audience and marketing goals.

Program: "Will my radio station be included in your recommendations?" If the answer to that question was affirmative, then I would discuss with the prospect the process for exchanging contracts and purchase orders.

If the answer was negative or non-committal, my next step would be to revisit the closing principle to gain agreement, or possibly agree to disagree, about the validity of the closing principle. This question gives a prospect the opportunity to confirm what they will do as a result of the closing principle. It also gives them an opportunity to raise an objection or dictate the next steps in the closing process. Either way they are allowing me to continue engaging with the prospect to keep the sales process moving forward.

Promise: "The audience I defined will be there to receive your message in the format I described." If the prospect confirms that my station will be included in an upcoming advertising campaign, follows the program, which are the next steps to buying what I am selling, then this promise will be fulfilled. They'll deliver their message to an important audience, as it directly relates to their marketing goals.

Closing Simple Sales

Simple sales are situations that typically involve only one decision-maker, a tangible product, and a relatively low-cost price tag. Closing in these situations allows a salesperson to get a full buying commitment from one person in a relatively short time. These scenarios usually occur in retail selling environments, business-to-consumer transactions.

Simple Closes

Closing in simple selling situations allows a salesperson to get a full buying commitment from one person in a relatively short time.

Principle: The closing principle in simple sales needs to be based upon truth and a benefit statement. This benefit statement must summarize why the prospect needs what's being sold. Attached to every significant fact or truth about a product or service is a benefit. For example, the fact that the books I sold were nonfiction meant that the content was verifiable and useful for educating.

Any motivation to buy should come from the prospect's desire to receive the benefits. The motivation to buy should not come from a pushy, self-serving salesperson. As people selling God's way, we don't manipulate; we motivate, encourage, and instruct (see Proverbs 9:9, 1 Thessalonians 5:14, and 2 Timothy 4:2).

Program: In simple selling scenarios where we can typically get the buying commitment from one person, our closing program needs to instruct the prospect on how to complete the sale. In some cases, all they must do is go to a counter or website and complete the purchase. In some simple selling situations, we may ask a direct question such as, "Do you want to buy this today, because what's being sold is unquestionably needed?" We follow that question with instructions on how to pay for the product.

Promise: The closing promise in these situations should speak to fulfilling the prospect's desires for the features and benefits presented. Of course, what would be presented at this point should align with the prospect's real needs and not the need to fulfill any self-serving ambitions. We should not sell more than what the prospect truly needs or wants. Nor should we sell less than what's needed. As people selling God's way, our closing promise must reinforce our commitment to honesty, humanity, and humility (see Leviticus 19:35, Philippians 2:3–4, and Colossians 3:12).

Our Commitment

Selling God's way reinforces our commitment to honesty, humanity, and humility.

Example: Selling Books

Here is an example from my days selling books, a simple sale because one person could (and often did) make the decision to buy. Also, the price tag of this tangible product was less than $1,000. During the presentation, I would begin closing anytime I received buying signals in the form of impromptu agreements or in-depth questions that required me to expound upon the features and benefits of what I was selling.

Principle: "These books will delight and enlighten your entire family, leading you and your children to become better educated." My closing principle, the benefit statements, typically focused on the opportunity for more education and entertainment. This was the undeniable truth about the nonfiction books that I sold, and it was also the benefit most people wanted from owning the books.

Program: "To get these books, all you must do is give me a deposit today of twenty dollars or more. The more you pay now, the less you must pay when the books arrive. Just sign here; I take cash or checks." My closing program involved instructions as to how the prospect could take ownership of the books. It also ignited a sense of urgency, because it involved doing things immediately.

Promise: "I'll send you a postcard in the mail, so you'll know the exact date I'll return with your books. It takes four to six weeks. On the day I deliver the books, you can give me the remaining balance and start enjoying your books that same day." My closing promise always ended in statements that described when the buyer could take delivery of the books and begin reaping the benefits of ownership.

Closing Complex Sales

Scenarios that involve more than one decision-maker are typically complex selling situations, whether the product is tangible or intangible. I use the word *complex* because these prospects often use professional buyers or sophisticated buying procedures. Once I began conducting business-to-business sales transactions, most of my selling situations involved more than one decision-maker, which meant complex sales.

Most business-to-business selling situations are complex sales. Typically, three or more people representing different areas of concerns were involved in the process: professional buyers concerned with the technical aspects of what is being sold, executive buyers whose concerns center on the product's ability to deliver what is being promised, and client buyers, whose concerns focus on the economic impact of buying what is being sold.

We don't always have access to all the decision-makers in a complex sale during the closing process even if we had direct contact with them while prospecting or presenting what we sell. To overcome these closing handicaps, we need to prepare each person we can access during our closing process to pass along our information to other decision-makers. This gets accomplished by first securing a buying commitment from each person present during our closing process—a commitment that's in line with their role and level of responsibility. For example, if we have direct access and can close with a person overseeing the budget or economic aspects of purchasing our product, then we need to secure their buying commitment, then focus on what their discussions will be like with other decision-makers. We should guide them to deliver the closing principle, program, and promise just as we presented it to them.

Principle: The closing principle in complex selling situations must encompass the concerns of each decision-maker. The closing principle should focus on the technical, service, and economic aspects of what we sell in a concise, confident manner. However, and most importantly, the closing principle in complex sales must be based upon an agreed-upon truth, or verifiable facts, accepted by at least one decision-maker and the salesperson. This is not like the closing principle in simple selling scenarios, where the truth behind the closing principle can be implied or assumed.

Program: The closing program in these scenarios secures the buyer's commitment and confirms that our selling process is in sync with their buying process. Closing questions are typically used in complex selling situations.These questions ask the decision-makers we can access for their perspective on what we sell before a final buying decision is rendered. In our closing program, the questions must lead the buyers to communicate any objections held by them or any other decision-maker. We need the decision-makers present during our closing process to voice the concerns and possible objections of any decision-maker not present.

We may ask questions like, "Will you complete your part of the financial application by Friday?" or "Are you including my product in the submission to your boss?" Questions like these lead the prospect to affirm their buying commitment or assert an objection. Either way, we are moving them through the sales process, because we are at a point of either closing a decision-maker or uncovering an objection. The next stage in the sales process deals with overcoming objections.

Promise: The closing promise in complex selling scenarios should speak to fulfilling each decision-maker's specific need, whether they are present or not. Of course, each decision- maker's specific need should have been discovered and discussed during the prospecting and questioning stages of the sales process. The closing promise in complex sales is multifaceted, because these selling situations contain multiple decision-makers with multiple needs. So, our closing promise must address the concerns of all the decision-makers in a manner that demonstrates our ability to fulfill multiple needs that revolve around technical, service, and economic priorities.

Examples: Selling Advertising

Here is an example from my days selling advertising, business-to-business sales transactions. I would begin closing any time after I received purchasing signals in the form of unexpected but positive questions that required in-depth answers. In most cases, I began closing immediately after a presentation.

Professional Buyers

Let's begin with an example of how to close with ***professional buyers.***

Principle: "My radio station ranks second in your client's demographic, regarding the number of people that you can reach within a specific time frame. I've also put together a schedule that fits within your cost parameters." With professional media buyers, I would use declarative statements that asserted the truth about the radio station's ability to meet or exceed technical requirements. An elaborate closing principle was not needed, because meeting or exceeding technical requirements was most often indisputable. However, as I stated earlier the truth needed to be agreed upon and even verifiable if necessary.

If my station did not meet the technical requirements, then I needed to craft a closing principle that explained why my station should be included, despite not meeting a technical requirement. For example, I would say something like "The individual incomes and buying powers of our listeners, combined with the station's format, which is ideal for your client's message, should make the inclusion of my radio station in your next campaign cost-effective and wise, despite the station's inability to offer a schedule that fits within your cost parameters."

Program: "Will you be including my radio station in the submission to your client?" or "In addition to my radio station, what other stations are you considering buying?" or "Do you think the client will raise an objection to buying my radio station?" These are examples of questions I would pose to implement my closing program with professional buyers while selling advertising. Questions like these are asking the decision-maker for their perspective and likelihood to buy, before any final buying decision is rendered. As I stated earlier, the closing program in complex selling requires questions that confirm that your sales process is in sync with the prospect's buying process. Furthermore, it gives buyers an opportunity to affirm their buying commitment and raise any objections that they or others may hold.

Promise: "In buying my station, you'll be reaching adults between the ages of thirty-five to fifty-four, in a format that's advantageous for selling your product. My station will prove to be an ideal investment of your client's advertising budget." Thereafter, I would present a list of clients who have repeatedly purchased advertising from the radio station.

My closing promise with professional media buyers painted a picture of how purchasing advertising from me would be viewed as a wise decision. I wanted buyers to possess an inner peace about their decision to buy my radio station, because their decision needed to survive scrutiny as it passed through their buying process. My closing promise would be statements communicating that my radio station delivered a product that technically satisfied the desired specifications, as it provided the service needed. The summation of my closing promise had to point to my product as a wise investment of their client's advertising budget.

Executive Buyers

Next, let's consider how to close with ***executive buyers***.

Principle: "My station has been a news and information leader in this market for more than twenty years. We have hundreds of satisfied clients repeatedly doing business with us. I'm sure we can help in your quest to get customers because advertising messages on our radio station reach a well-educated adult audience in a format that is conducive to generating customers." In closing executive ad buyers, my principle focused on the radio station's ability to deliver customers, because most executives would take a bottom-line approach to buying advertising. They primarily needed an advertising service that helped to bring in customers and enrich their company's popularity and profitability. So, I would make statements about how our listeners responded to the radio station's commercial messages and how the station worked for similar clients regarding generating customers.

I mostly sold advertising for talk and news radio stations, so my closing principle relied on the fact that people listened to those formats more attentively. This enabled commercials to blend into the format in ways that transferred credibility to their advertising message.

Program: "What do you want the next step in the process to be?" or "If you're okay with what I presented, I'll show this to [insert name] at your company," or "If you don't have any objections, can we begin on [date]?" The closing program for executive buyers consisted of questions that, when answered, revealed their likelihood to purchase, along with their perspective on the next step in the process. The closing program that I presented offered executives a way to verify that my sales process was in sync with their buying process.

Promise: "We can begin your advertising on [insert date]. Rest assured that the station's audience includes a significant portion of people in your needed demographic. You're advertising in a medium that continues to work well, which means it continues to be a wise investment for all the advertisers." The closing promise with executive buyers recapped how purchasing the advertising met the needs of all the decision-makers. The promise was also positioned as if there were no more objections to buying the radio station. In most cases, I'd use the same closing promise that I used with the professional buyer. If needed, I would add statements that in effect promised that they were advertising on a radio station that had worked well for many other clients.

Client Buyers

Finally, let's consider how to close with client buyers.

Principle: "The radio station delivers an audience that matches the profile of your potential customers in a format proven to be advantageous for numerous clients." Of course, with every buyer, I would go into a lot more detail about the audience, format, and current list of repeat clients. The closing principle with client buyers comes out of the issues discussed during the questioning stage of the sales process. In this example, the closing principle needed to articulate how buying advertising from me exemplified a wise investment, as it directly related to their needs and expectations. My closing principle had to arise out of a concrete conviction that my product had the components needed to fulfill that prospect's specific needs and expectations.

Sometimes, I encountered difficulty establishing a closing principle with client buyers; usually, this occurred when buyers had unrealistic expectations. In those instances, the buyer needed more education as to how advertising worked, which I had typically already tried to accomplish during an earlier stage of the sales process. If I was unable to get an expectation revised, then my closing principle needed to communicate an honest assessment of the outcome I anticipated.

I would not craft a close that catered to the questionable expectations of a potential client, which would be misleading and open the door to customer dissatisfaction. Because the buyer would be expecting a result that I could not promise or guarantee. As a person selling God's way, I needed to resist the temptation to abandon my beliefs to close a sale. For example, I had some clients who stated that they needed twelve phone calls per week from my advertising to justify the expenditure. Other clients stated they needed numerous customers in their store saying they heard about their business through the radio ads to rationalize spending advertising dollars with me. As a person selling righteously, my closing principle could not be based on claiming to satisfy such unrealistic expectations.

When we sell God's way, our closing principle must be based on truth and not on any wishes or fortuity. So, in those situations, my closing principle needed to be statements of truth that essentially said, "I don't know if that's going to happen as a result of your advertising on the station, but I do know this is the right radio station for your marketing message," or "It's very difficult for any advertising vehicle to predict those types of results. But we do have hundreds of advertisers who sign repeat contracts, because of the results my station delivers."

Program: "When do you want to start?" or "What commercial will you be using?" or "How many weeks do you want your commercials to air?" While selling advertising, my closing program with client buyers consisted of assumptive questions that presupposed the client intended to buy. The answers to those questions allowed me to instruct the buyer as to what they needed to do to finalize the sale. As people selling God's way, we should always expect blessings to flow our way (see Psalm 23:6).

Promise: "The radio station delivers the right audience in the right environment. We can help with your challenge with raising awareness and weekend traffic. The radio station has worked well for a good number of advertisers. I'm committed to doing all I can for your campaign to be successful." The closing promise with client buyers was much like the closing promise with professional and executive buyers. It recapped how purchasing the radio advertising met the needs of all the buyers. It also summarized why they could have an inner peace about their decision to buy advertising from me. Much like all closing promises, it predicted the outcome if the prospect adhered to the principle and followed the program. At the same time, the closing promise must communicate something that the prospect views as vital to solving a problem or capitalizing on an opportunity.

Obstacles to Closing

- *Fear*: Fear of rejection or failure can prevent any of us from closing sales. By embracing God's Word, which says over 300 times, "Do not fear," we will overcome being afraid in any situation. As believers in Jesus Christ as Lord and Savior, we can find the courage to go through any closing process successfully, regardless of any past failures. God will meet all our needs and never leave us wanting. This obviously covers our career and financial needs. Holding to this truth will allow us to push forward, closing aggressively and disregarding fear in any selling scenario (see Joshua 1:7 and Psalm 23:1–4).

Fear can also lead us to close sales unrighteously, as we attempt to sell something not needed or wanted, out of a self-serving desire for money or status. For people selling God's way, it's far more important to sell righteously in a manner that aligns with God's Word than to make sales unrighteously in a manner that is self-serving, neglecting the needs of others and biblical wisdom.

- *Inexperience*: The most harmful result of being an inexperienced salesperson lies in the inability to close sales. Inexperienced salespeople generally don't know how to articulate appropriate closing principles, programs, and promises. Fortunately, believers have Jesus, and He said that He would be with us always. When faced with selling situations where inexperience may cost us a sale, we need to simply rely on the teachings of Jesus. We should embrace prayer, Bible study, and godly counsel for righteous instructions that help us close successfully. As a teacher and helper, Jesus is far more valuable than anything that we can gain through experience. The Gospel of John says that if we remain in Jesus and His words remain in us, we can ask for whatever we wish, and it will be done (see John 15:7).

- *Objections*: An objection is an obstacle to closing a sale. To overcome objections, we must gain an honest assessment of what's occurring from the buyer's point of view. This starts by gaining a complete understanding of what the objection is and why it exists. I cover objections extensively in the next chapter. What we learn about an objection gives us the freedom to aggressively continue or discontinue closing sales, being confident that either way, we're reacting to an objection righteously (see John 8:31–32).

More Valuable Than Experience

When faced with selling situations where inexperience may cost us a sale, we need to simply rely on the teachings of Jesus. We should embrace prayer, Bible study, and godly counsel for righteous instructions that help us close successfully. As a teacher and helper, Jesus is far more valuable than anything we gain through experience.

Questions

1. After your presentation, what steps are needed to complete the sale? Are these steps obvious and logical?

2. Do you have a closing conscience, an instinctual motivation that always drives you to deliver those closing words, be they statements, instructions, or questions? How does this motivation affect both you and your prospects?

3. What is your closing promise? Does it predict the outcome if the prospect adheres to the principle and follows the program?

4. Does your closing promise communicate something that the prospect views as vital to solving a problem or capitalizing on an opportunity?

Scriptural References

- Jesus commands His disciples to go and make disciples:

  Then Jesus came to them and said, "All authority in Heaven and on earth has been given to me. Therefore go and make disciples of all nations, baptizing them in the name of the Father and of the Son and of the Holy Spirit" (Matthew 28:18–19).

- Jesus commends those who did not witness His earthly mission yet still follow Him:

  Then Jesus told him, "Because you have seen me, you have believed; blessed are those who have not seen and yet have believed" (John 20:29).

- As people selling God's way, we don't manipulate; we motivate, encourage, and instruct:

  Instruct the wise and they will be wiser still; teach the righteous and they will add to their learning (Proverbs 9:9).

  And we urge you, brothers and sisters, warn those who are idle and disruptive, encourage the disheartened, help the weak, be patient with everyone (1 Thessalonians 5:14).

  Preach the word; be prepared in season and out of season; correct, rebuke and encourage—with great patience and careful instruction (2 Timothy 4:2).

- Selling righteously reinforces our commitment to honesty, humanity, and humility:

  Do not use dishonest standards when measuring length, weight or quantity (Leviticus 19:35).

  Do nothing out of selfish ambition or vain conceit. Rather, in humility value others above yourselves, not looking to your own interests but each of you to the interests of others (Philippians 2:3–4).

  Therefore, as God's chosen people, holy and dearly loved, clothe yourselves with compassion, kindness, humility, gentleness and patience (Colossians 3:12).

- As people selling God's way, we should always expect blessings to flow our way:

  Surely goodness and love will follow me all the days of my life, and I will dwell in the house of the L*ORD* *forever* (Psalm 23:6).

- Embracing the Word of God allows us to overcome fears:

  Be strong and very courageous. Be careful to obey all the law my servant Moses gave you; do not turn from it to the right or to the left, that you may be successful wherever you go (Joshua 1:7).

- As believers in Jesus Christ as Lord and Savior, we will never want for anything. Obviously, this covers our career and financial wants. This allows us to push forward, closing aggressively and disregarding fear in any selling situation:

  The L*ORD* *is my shepherd, I lack nothing. He makes me lie down in green pastures, he leads me beside quiet waters, he refreshes my soul. He guides me along right paths for his name's sake. Even though I walk through the darkest valley, I will fear no evil; for you are with me; your rod and your staff, they comfort me* (Psalm 23:1–4).

- Even with selling, Jesus is a far better teacher and helper than experience:

  "*If you remain in me and my words remain in you, ask whatever you wish, and it will be done for you*" (John 15:7).

- Embracing truth gives us the freedom to close sales aggressively:

  To the Jews who had believed him, Jesus said, "If you hold to my teaching, you are really my disciples. Then you will know the truth, and the truth will set you free" (John 8:31–32).

CHAPTER 9:

Objections

Consider it pure joy, my brothers and sisters, whenever you face trials of many kinds, because you know that the testing of your faith produces perseverance. Let perseverance finish its work so that you may be mature and complete, not lacking anything. If any of you lacks wisdom, you should ask God, who gives generously to all without finding fault, and it will be given to you. But when you ask, you must believe and not doubt, because the one who doubts is like a wave of the sea, blown and tossed by the wind. That person should not expect to receive anything from the Lord. Such a person is double-minded and unstable in all they do.

—James 1:2–8

Trials and Testing

In AD 49, Jesus's brother James wrote one of the best books ever on Christian living. In the first chapter, he says that we'll face trials of many kinds. As salespeople, the trials we face most often come in the form of objections. An objection exists whenever a prospect has a reason for stopping the sales process. Objections can occur at any time: they foil first meetings, keep questions from being answered, prevent prospects from attending presentations, and cancel commitments that could close sales.

Objections are either communicated, becoming known and visible, or uncommunicated, remaining unknown or imperceptible. Communicated objections can help to continue the sales process by inviting resolution. Whenever a prospect communicates an objection, we should view this as an opportunity to overcome the objection and uncover any uncommunicated objections. Communicated objections can also completely stop the sales process by becoming more important than any reason to buy.

Uncommunicated objections can completely stop the sales process, because the invitation to resolve an objection never arrives. However, sales processes can continue with uncommunicated objections if a reason to buy overpowers the objection, dissolving its ability to stop the sales process. Our trial as wise sellers lies in doing the righteous thing so that all objections get resolved, refuted, or dissolved.

Handle Objections Righteously

Our trial as wise sellers lies in doing the righteous things so that all objections get resolved, refuted, or dissolved.

James instructs believers to count all trials (or in our case, objections) as joy, because they come to test our faith and produce perseverance. He says this perseverance must finish its work so that we become mature and complete, not lacking anything. As people selling God's way, we should rejoice when objections surface because they help us examine our beliefs, revealing what we really rely on.

This testing of our faith makes us more competent sellers, not lacking anything to be successful. If we place our faith in God, we rely on Him to lead us to the best thing to say or do in overcoming any objection. God will lead us to use skills and resources that we possess but have not accessed. He will also direct us to develop new skills and ways of doing things as we strive to overcome objections and become righteously competent, successful salespeople.

Overcoming Objections

Whenever a prospect stops or stalls a sales process, it's because of one or more objections, which may be communicated or uncommunicated. However, our needs as salespeople require us to complete sales processes, stopping or stalling a sales process only when we deem it necessary. We must overcome any objection from a prospect, then restart the sales process. Successfully completing this challenge flows from an honest examination of a prospect and the current sales process. Whenever a prospect presents an objection, indicating that they will not be buying, or by procrastinating, preventing the sales process from progressing, we need to ask them why. Doing this starts an examination of the sales process.

With communicated objections, we examine the prospects' answers as to why the sales process can't go forward. With uncommunicated objections, we must examine why the sales process stopped from another perspective. We can look back upon all that has occurred during the sales process or seek godly counsel from another person to gain a better perspective of our selling situation. We may find the reason why an uncommunicated objection stopped the sales process through social media or published industry news. For example, we may uncover via social media or a new source that executives and the priorities in the company have changed, or that a new technology has brought about a company shift regarding goals and focus.

James also says in the first chapter of his book on Christian living, "*Do not be deceived.*" Asking "why" questions places the entire sales process under scrutiny, so neither we nor our prospects get deceived. Under righteous scrutinization, we can ask even more questions to determine the validity of the objection and uncover concealed objections that may contain the real reason why the sales process stopped. We're questioning to gain an understanding of what the objection is, why it exists, and why it ended our sales process. We need to find out if an objection arises out of facts, opinions, or misconceptions. We also need to discern the prospect's veracity. Our conclusions about the prospect's integrity will guide us as we attempt to overcome objections, leading us to confront prospects to refute or ignore objections. Our goal is to prevent the objection from halting or hindering our sales process (see James 1:16).

Discover Truth

We need to find out if an objection arises out of facts, opinions, or misconceptions. We also need to discern the prospect's veracity.

While asking "why" questions, we can begin overcoming objections by resolving any concerns that brought about the objection, refuting the perceived validity of the objection, or dissolving any importance attached to the objection. We do this by using the truth about what we sell and how we sell it; this tactic calls for an honest examination of what's been occurring in all aspects of the sales process.

We must examine every phase of the sales process for righteousness and thoroughness. We need to review how we prospected for this potential buyer: Hopefully, we dug deep enough to find the right type of potential customer and are interacting with this prospect based on biblical principles. We must analyze the questioning stage of this sales process, knowing that we needed to gather enough of the right type of information to create a passionate, persuasive presentation. We need to dissect the presentation delivered to ensure that the solution presented helped to solve a problem or maximize an opportunity. Our presentation should also have met specific needs and been presented alongside a vision of the future that communicated a complete understanding of the client's situation. We must review our closing actions, hoping to see a high-quality closing principle, program, and promise—a closing principle that expressed a truth that we undoubtedly hold about our product or service that's directly related to meeting that prospect's specific needs.

The closing program should have sparked a sense of urgency, as it instructed or affirmed the action steps needed to complete the purchase, and it should have included a closing promise that predicted the outcome if the prospect adhered to the principle and followed the program.

It's important to note that we can question prospects to clarify what's been happening during the sales process. Input from prospects can be illuminating. If we discover discrepancies during our dissection of the sales process, then as people selling God's way, we need to repent and begin again, restarting the sales process at the point we strayed from selling righteously. However, if we do not detect any deviations from selling righteously, then we need to continue overcoming objections by resolving concerns, refuting validity and dissolving importance.

Resolving Concerns

Concerns come as conditions cropping up out of a prospect's anxiety, distrust, or fear. Prospects may communicate fear that the price is too high, the quality too low, the quantity too small, or the commitment too long. We'll hear things that generally mean they want more (or less) of something we offer. We resolve concerns by making additions or subtractions to what we offer. This alleviates the concerns that created the objection, erasing any condition that caused the sales process to cease.

Biblical Examples of Resolving Concerns

In the Bible's first sales transaction, which I featured in chapter 4, Jacob's distrust of Esau created an objection that could have completely stopped their sales process. Because Jacob did not trust Esau, he needed him to do more than just hand over the birthright; he needed him to swear it over first. Of course, Esau did swear it over first, resolving Jacob's trust issue, which allowed the sales process to continue (see Genesis 25:33).

During God's presentation to Moses at the burning bush, which I featured in chapter 10, Moses's fears about being slow of speech and tongue caused him to be concerned about his ability to lead the Israelites out of Egypt. God resolved Moses's concerns by lessening his responsibility and sending Aaron (Moses's brother) to assist. And God told Moses that He Himself would help him speak and teach him what to do (see Exodus 4:10–15).

My Examples of Resolving Concerns

Two objections I faced most often while selling advertising concerned the price ("too high") and the ratings ("too low"). These price objections were rooted in anxieties related to overspending (as if purchasing my product stole the money needed for far more important matters). To alleviate the anxieties associated with this objection, I would simply find a way to lower the price. This resulted in me selling a schedule for ten weeks instead of thirteen, or a schedule with twenty commercials per week instead of twenty-five. This dropped the cost to a level that still allowed me to offer a service capable of solving problems or maximizing an opportunity. This also allowed the client to buy within budget, so funds remained available for other needs.

The prospect's ratings objections were rooted in fears that the number of people in my station's audience was too small to help them achieve their advertising goals (as if purchasing my product pummeled profits, because only a paltry number of people might respond to their marketing message). My approach to resolving these types of objections involved the use of give-and-take scenarios. So, with this objection, I would add more of what I was selling by presenting more facts and features. I would share facts in the form of research that showed the audience's propensity to purchase their product. I added a promotional element capable of generating an even greater response to an ad campaign—things such as an enter-to-win sweepstakes or a gift-with-purchase program.

Give and Take

We resolve concerns by making additions or subtractions to what we sell or how we sell it. This alleviates the concern that created the objection and eliminates the condition that caused the sales process to cease.

My goal was to offer things that gave the radio station's audience an opportunity to verify their inclination to respond favorably to the prospect's marketing message, in exchange for the prospect taking away their objection, which had halted the sales process. I also wanted to correct expectations and erase fears by educating the prospect on the power of radio advertising, allowing the client to go forward with a more empowering and less encumbering view of what they were buying. Radio stations can help not only by airing a client's commercials to an audience of qualified potential buyers, which at the very least raises awareness of who they are and what they offer. But radio stations can also serve their advertisers by incorporating a client's marketing message into promotions and contests done by the station or their on-air personalities to help generate more tangible results.

Refuting Validity

During our examination of why an objection exists and why it extinguished our sales process, we may discover objections rooted in untruths. Prospects may hold incorrect assumptions, believing a competitor's product is better or that our product can't meet their needs. We may also hear concerns related to price and prior use, things like "We can't afford your services" or "We used similar services in the past that proved to be ineffective." To refute these objections, we must present the facts about what we sell and how we sell it, along with evidence that substantiates those facts. The evidence we present must be in direct opposition to the ignorance, illogic, or irrelevance that gave birth to these objections. Our goal is to invalidate the fundamental reason behind why this objection exists.

Biblical Examples of Refuting Validity

A group of religious leaders called Sadducees were in staunch opposition to Jesus and His teaching. As Jesus went about saving souls, the Sadducees would confront Him with objections in the form of questions designed to derail His ministry. On one such occasion, the Sadducees questioned Jesus about death and marriage at the resurrection. Jesus's reply, which is factual and found in the Gospel of Matthew, simply says, "*You are in error because you do not know the Scripture or the power of God.*"

In reading the entire passage, we see that Jesus simply uses the Holy Scripture to substantiate His statements and expose the

Sadducees' ignorance. At the end of this biblical story, it notes that the crowds were astonished at Jesus's teaching, making the objection the Sadducees raised to trample Jesus's teaching assist Him in saving souls for God's Kingdom (see Matthew 22:29–33).

In the book of Acts, circumcised Christians criticized Peter for entering the home of an uncircumcised Christian. Their criticism surfaces as an objection to Peter's legitimacy in leading the church. Peter's reply was to logically explain why he entered the home and what he did while there. To corroborate his account, Peter pointed to six other men who went with him who could testify to the truth he spoke. At the end of this biblical story, we are told that after hearing all Peter had to say, the circumcised Christians had no further objections (see Acts 11:1–18).

Truth Triumphs

To refute and remove objections rooted in untruths, we present the facts about what we sell and how we sell it along with evidence that substantiates those facts.

My Examples of Refuting Validity

While selling advertising, the two objections that I frequently needed to refute were "The competitor's product is better," and "I don't need to advertise." These erroneous objections most often occurred during the prospecting or questioning stage of the sales process. The objection about the competitor was rooted in ignorance because the prospect assumed they possessed an adequate understanding of what I sold and how it compared to the competition (even though they never witnessed an accurate side-by-side comparison of the two products). Their assumption arose out of faulty information supplied by the competition or some other refutable source. The "I don't need to advertise" objection typically sprang out of an illogical, ill-founded view of business and marketing as if the reality of business cycles, unpredictable buyer behavior, and competition didn't affect their company, affording them the enviable position of not having to advertise for new customers or campaign for old customers to return.

To combat these objections, I would present the benefits of what I sold, along with accurate comparisons. For prospects who thought I was selling something inferior to the competition, I would present a side-by-side comparison of both products and services. For the "I don't need to advertise" objections, I would present a comparison of companies that did advertise and those that didn't. My success in refuting these objections resided in how much light and salt I could bring into the situation (light being the truth about what I sold, and the salt being how tastefully I could educate the prospect, while pointing out their ignorance or illogic). As a person selling God's way, I'm required to bring salt and light into all situations (see Matthew 5:13–16 and Colossians 4:6).

Dissolving Importance

Some objections are so inconsequential that they need to be ignored or improved. Prospects may communicate things they learned through rumor or rudimentary reading. We may hear assertions and claims that reflect a lack of intelligence or interest. Claims that may start with words like "I read that . . ." or "My friend/spouse/neighbor said that . . ." To dissolve these insignificant objections, we must shift the conversation toward the needs of the prospect and the facts associated with what we sell. Redirecting the sales conversation this way can be accomplished through questions that focus on their needs or closing statements that cite specific benefits of our product or service. This refocuses the prospect's thinking toward the sales process and overwhelms any inconsequential objection. Ignoring these objections and steering the conservation toward truth allows the prospect to either bury or build up their own objection.

If prospects continue objecting by adding substance to their initial assertions, then we need to refute or resolve the objection in one of the manners previously discussed. However, most objections rooted in rumors, innuendoes, and irrelevancies get buried as the truth surfaces. Practically all uncommunicated insignificant objections get buried by truth, as the needs of a prospect and the facts associated with what we sell surface.

Biblical Examples of Dissolving Importance

Another group of religious leaders opposing Jesus's ministry was called the Pharisees. They too would confront Jesus with objections to his ministry. On one occasion, the Pharisees and Sadducees approached Jesus, asking for a heavenly sign to prove that He was Christ, as if a sign from heaven would remove any objection they had to following Him. Jesus clearly possessed the power to present a sign but chose not to. Instead, He redirected the Pharisees and Sadducees to the facts about the people of a wicked and adulterous generation. At the end this confrontation, Jesus referred to the fact that He would be crucified and rise again, a truth that would bring salvation to all who put their faith in Jesus. Then He left the Pharisees and Sadducees to continue His ministry, without giving an answer to their objection (see Matthew 16:1–4).

Turn toward Truth

To dissolve insignificant objections, we must redirect the conversation toward the needs of the prospect and the facts associated with what we sell.

The Bible also contains the story of Stephen, the first person to die for the gospel. He was a man full of God's grace and power. Stephen converted a noteworthy number of Jews to Christianity. The book of Acts says that he performed marvelous works and miracles. Members of a synagogue produced false witnesses to end Stephen's ministry. They accused him of degrading the temple and disregarding the customs of Moses. The Sanhedrin, a council of judges, seized Stephen, seeking to substantiate those accusations. Stephen's reply to the Sanhedrin didn't include any mention of the accusations. Instead, he spoke about Jewish history and the persecution of prophets, revealing his commitment to the faith and his knowledge of historical facts. Stephen's presentation to the Sanhedrin led to his martyrdom, making him a hero who helped to convert countless numbers to Christianity after his death (see Acts 6:8–14).

My Example of Dissolving Importance

The inconsequential objections I faced most often centered on credibility. A prospect would claim that investing in radio advertising didn't deliver customers, despite the overwhelming evidence that radio advertising worked, given the abundance of popular radio stations and the numerous prospering radio advertisers. My reply was to redirect the conversation toward the prospect's needs and the facts associated with radio advertising. Defusing objections this way allowed me to continue the sales process by transitioning from prospecting to questioning about needs or from questioning to presenting benefits about the advertising time I was selling. As I mentioned earlier, these types of objections typically occur near the prospecting or questioning stage of the sales process. My strategy was to refocus the conversation toward legitimate reasons to buy, which were far more important than any inconsequential objection I just ignored.

Testing Our Faith

Objections come to test our faith. Second Corinthians says we must examine ourselves to see if we operate in the faith. As believers, our faith should be in God, trusting in Him to supply all our needs. Because of our faith, our actions must present proof that Jesus lives as Lord of our life and that the Word of God (Bible) serves to direct our behavior. Our behavior in overcoming objections must reflect the character of a faithful person. If we use things like an honest assessment of our actions and repentance of unrighteous behavior to overcome objections, then we provide proof that our commitment to success flows through faithfulness (see 2 Corinthians 13:5).

In an honest examination of our selling behavior, we may discover a combination of things done correctly and incorrectly. We must use what we learn to become more skillful at selling, discarding what's unrighteous, improving what's needed, and duplicating what's righteous. In this way, we persist toward our goal of becoming faithful people who sell God's way by using the testing of our faith to develop a process that allows us to persevere and progress. This same process allows us to develop a deeper relationship with Jesus Christ, as we depend upon our faith in Him for guidance and growth while selling.

Objections can also reveal what we must learn, and they help us apply what we learn as people of faith. In chapter 2, I discussed the Bible's first sales transaction, emphasizing that we need to become skillful to be successful, like Esau, who became a skillful hunter and a successful salesman. Learning how to use the tools of faith and progressing in the use of those tools provides additional proof that our commitment to success flows through faith. The most prominent tools of faith are fasting, fellowshipping with other believers, giving, serving, praying, praising, and studying the Bible. Of course, we can do all these things while selling or preparing to sell.

Mature and Complete

This method of receiving, analyzing, and overcoming objections requires a systematic way of thinking. Mastering this thought process gives us a tool to use whenever a prospect stops or stalls our sales process. The more adept we become at using this thought process, the more adept we'll be at skillfully soaring through the sales process and swiftly confronting objections to say or do the right thing so they are resolved, refuted, or dissolved. The persuasion phase of selling doesn't begin until we encounter an objection. At that point, we need to overcome the objection and complete the sale, which requires that we persuade prospects that their objections are insignificant or irresolvable.

The more objections we encounter, the more proficient we'll become at persuading. The genetic composition of every successful salesperson contains the power to persuade. That's why we should rejoice when objections arrive because they come to make us mature and complete salespeople, able to persuade in a variety of selling scenarios. In that way, we are not lacking anything needed for a successful sales career. As we see in James 1:4, perseverance must finish its work so that we can become "*mature and complete, not lacking anything.*"

Celebrate Objections

We should rejoice when objections are raised because handling them makes us mature and complete salespeople able to persuade in a variety of selling situations.

Insurmountable Objections

James chapter 1 says that if any of us lacks wisdom, we should ask God for it and not doubt that He will give it to us. So, we need to ask God for the wisdom to conquer or concede to objections, and then remain alert so that we can adhere to God's answer. The primary ways God speaks to us are through His Word and the Holy Spirit.

There were instances when godly wisdom revealed to me that an objection merited stopping the sales process. At times, I found prospects without the capital, urgency, or authority to buy what I sold. Sometimes, I discovered that the competitor's product was better; in those selling scenarios, I promptly and politely stopped selling. This allowed me to continue building a righteous relationship that could help close sales later as the prospect returned in a better position to buy. Keep in mind that one of our goals is not necessarily to close sales, but to open relationships from which sales spring forth.

Preventing Objections

There is a direct correlation between decreasing the number of objections that we receive and increasing the number of satisfied clients. The more mature and complete we become as salespeople, the better we'll be at preventing objections and creating satisfied clients. When we search for customers, we'll be more astute at qualifying prospects and orchestrating meetings. During the questioning, we'll be better at analyzing situations, establishing righteous relationships, and discovering significant needs. Our presentations will include more useful solutions, wrapped in more valuable visions of the future. Finally, the action we undertake to get a buying commitment will come with more concrete closing principles, programs, and promises. This will be followed by superior customer service spun through our commitment to sell righteously.

Questions

1. What are the three objections you most typically encounter? How can you prevent these objections from occurring?

2. Have objections helped you become a better salesperson? If yes, how? If not, why not?

3. Do you pray to God, seeking the wisdom and words to overcome specific objections? If yes, why? If you do not, why not?

Scriptural References

- We should examine our actions and the prospect's behavior, so we will not be deceived:

  Don't be deceived, my dear brothers and sisters (James 1:16).

- Esau resolved Jacob's trust issue; this allowed the sales process to continue:

  But Jacob said, "Swear to me first." So he swore an oath to him, selling his birthright to Jacob (Genesis 25:33).

- God resolved Moses's fears by lessening his responsibility by sending Aaron to help:

  Moses said to the Lord, "Pardon your servant, Lord, I have never been eloquent, neither in the past nor since you have spoken to your servant. I am slow of speech and tongue." The LORD *said to him, "Who gave human beings their mouths? Who makes them deaf or mute? Who gives them sight or makes them blind? Is it not I, the* LORD*? Now go; I will help you speak and will teach you what to say." But Moses said, "Pardon your servant, Lord, please send someone else."*

Then the LORD*'s anger burned against Moses and he said, "What about your brother, Aaron the Levite? I know he can speak well. He is already on his way to meet you, and his heart will be glad when he sees you. You shall speak to him and put words in his mouth; I will help both of you speak and will teach you what to do"* (Exodus 4:10–15).

- Jesus refuted the validity of questions posed by the Sadducees, using Scripture to substantiate His statements:

Jesus replied, "You are in error because you do not know the Scriptures or the power of God. At the resurrection people will neither marry nor be given in marriage; they will be like the angels in heaven. But about the resurrection of the dead—have you not read what God said to you, 'I am the God of Abraham, the God of Isaac, and the God of Jacob. He is not the God of the dead but of the living.'" When the crowds heard this, they were astonished at his teaching (Matthew 22:29–33).

- Peter used truth and logic to resolve the objections coming from circumcised Christians:

The apostles and the believers throughout Judea heard that the Gentiles also had received the word of God. So when Peter went up to Jerusalem, the circumcised believers criticized him and said, "You went into the house of uncircumcised men and ate with them." Peter began and explained everything to them precisely as it had happened: "I was in the city of Joppa praying, and in a trance I saw a vision. I saw something like a large sheet being let down from heaven by its four corners, and it came down to where I was. I looked into it and saw four-footed animals of the earth, wild beasts, reptiles, and birds of the air. Then I heard a voice telling me, 'Get up, Peter. Kill and eat.' I replied, 'Surely not, Lord! Nothing impure or unclean has ever entered my mouth.' The voice spoke from heaven a second time, 'Do not call anything impure that God has made clean.' This happened three times, and then it was all pulled up to heaven again.

Right then three men who had been sent to me from Caesarea stopped at the house where I was staying. The Spirit told me to have no hesitation about going with them. These six brothers also went with me, and we entered the man's house. He told us how he had seen an angel appear in his house and say, 'Send to Joppa for Simon who is called Peter. He will bring you a message through which you and all your household will be saved.' As I began to speak, the Holy Spirit came on them as he had come on us at the beginning. Then I remembered what the Lord had said: 'John baptized with water, but you will be baptized with the Holy Spirit.' So if God gave them the same gift as he gave us, who believed in the Lord Jesus Christ, who was I to think that I could oppose God?" When they heard this, they had no further objections and praised God, saying, "So then, God has granted even the Gentiles repentance unto life" (Acts 11:1–18).

- As a person selling God's way, I am required to bring salt and light into all situations (light being the truth about what I sell, and salt being the tasteful way I overcome objections):

  You are the salt of the earth. But if the salt loses its saltiness, how can it be made salty again? It is no longer good for anything, except to be thrown out and trampled by men. You are the light of the world. A city on a hill cannot be hidden. Neither do people light a lamp and put it under a bowl. Instead they put it on its stand, and it gives light to everyone in the house. In the same way, let your light shine before men, that they may see your good deeds and praise your Father in heaven (Matthew 5:13–16).

  Let your conversation be always full of grace, seasoned with salt, so that you may know how to answer everyone (Colossians 4:6).

- Jesus defused the importance of a request that surfaced as an objection. The Pharisees and Sadducees asked Jesus for a sign from heaven to remove any objections they had to following Him:

  The Pharisees and Sadducees came to Jesus and tested him by asking him to show them a sign from heaven. He replied, "When evening comes, you say, 'It will be fair weather, for the sky is red,' and in the morning, 'Today it will be stormy, for the sky is red and overcast.' You know how to interpret the appearance of the sky, but you cannot interpret the signs of the times. A wicked and adulterous generation looks for a miraculous sign, but none will be given it except the sign of Jonah." Jesus then left them and went away (Matthew 16:1–4).

- Members of a synagogue opposed Stephen through charges coming from false witnesses and accusations he completely ignored during his presentation to the Sanhedrin:

  Now Stephen, a man full of God's grace and power, did great wonders and miraculous signs among the people. Opposition arose, however, from members of the Synagogue of the Freedmen (as it was called)—Jews of Cyrene and Alexandria as well as the provinces of Cilicia and Asia. These men began to argue with Stephen, but they could not stand up against his wisdom or the Spirit by whom he spoke. Then they secretly persuaded some men to say, "We have heard Stephen speak words of blasphemy against Moses and against God." So they stirred up the people and the elders and the teachers of the law. They seized Stephen and brought him before the Sanhedrin. They produced false witnesses, who testified, "This fellow never stops speaking against this holy place and against the law. For we have heard him say that this Jesus of Nazareth will destroy this place and change the customs Moses handed down to us" (Acts 6:8–14).

- Objections are calls to examine ourselves to see if we operate in the faith:

  Examine yourselves as to whether you are in the faith; test yourselves. Do you not realize that Jesus Christ is in you—unless, of course, you fail the test (2 Corinthians 13:5).

CHAPTER 10:

Service

Then he [Eliezer] *prayed, "Lord, God of my master Abraham, make me successful today, and show kindness to my master Abraham. See, I am standing beside this spring, and the daughters of the townspeople are coming out to draw water. May it be that when I say to a girl, 'Please let down your jar that I may have a drink,' and she says, 'Drink, and I'll water your camels too,' let her be the one you have chosen for your servant Isaac. By this I will know that you have shown kindness to my master."*

Before he had finished praying, Rebekah came out with her jar on her shoulder. She was the daughter of Bethuel son of Milcah, who was the wife of Abraham's brother Nahor. The girl was very beautiful, a virgin; no man had ever slept with her. She went down to the spring, filled her jar and came up again. The servant hurried to meet her and said, "Please give me a little water from your jar." "Drink, my lord," she said, and quickly lowered the jar to her hands and gave him a drink. After she had given him a drink, she said, "I'll draw water for your camels too, until they have had enough to drink." So she quickly emptied her jar into the trough, ran back to the well to draw more water, and drew enough for all his camels.

—Genesis 24:12–20

Eliezer and Rebekah

These events of more than four thousand years ago give us an example of how to deliver superior customer service. In this story, Eliezer (Abraham's chief servant) and Rebekah (the future wife of Abraham's son) both acted righteously to serve others. Eliezer's actions sprang out of Abraham's instructions. Abraham gave Eliezer explicit instructions for finding a wife for his son Isaac. Without hesitating, Eliezer focused on following those instructions, while also praying for success. Rebekah's actions arose out of a more natural instinctive desire to serve. Immediately after Eliezer asked for water, Rebekah responded rapidly to his request. Next, she anticipated his camels' thirst and quickly served them water as well.

Through Eliezer's prayer and Rebekah's swiftness, we see two people serving without complaining or compromising. They both possessed the right attitude for delivering superior service, that attitude being a mindset to meet the needs of others without giving priority to any personal pain or plans. We also see two people serving by responding to instructions quickly and working faithfully to meet and anticipate needs. One had a plan to serve, and the other had a passion for serving, but both had an ardent desire to meet the needs of others using the righteous resources at hand.

The seven righteous resources Eliezer and Rebekah used to deliver superior service during those early biblical days are the same things needed to deliver excellent service today.

Seven Righteous Resources Needed for Superior Service

Righteous Attitude

Delivering superior service starts by embracing the right attitude, a mindset that motivates us to satisfy the needs of others regardless of any personal pain or plans. Throughout all of history, the best example of this will forever be Jesus, who said that He came to serve and not to be served. He willingly served through suffering a ghastly death on the cross, taking the punishment for our sins (see Mark 10:45).

A righteous attitude toward service should be exemplified throughout the entire sales process. As soon as we start selling, our commitment to learning selling techniques and processes should intensify as an expression of our attitude to deliver righteous results in an excellent manner. Our righteous attitude becomes even more impactful, if we continually persist in learning selling skills, customer insights, and product knowledge. This goes well beyond what was learned during the initial stages of our sales careers because market conditions and customer needs evolve, and we always want to be empowered and equipped to deliver superior customer service.

Pain and Plans

Delivering superior service starts by embracing the right attitude, a mindset that motivates us to satisfy the needs of others regardless of any personal pain or plans.

As we search for customers, a righteous attitude toward serving others is verified by the prospects we discard. The process for finding the right type of customer requires us to dig deep through an immense amount of information, as we contact numerous individuals. At times, this can be taxing and frustrating, leading us to latch on to prospects who may be accessible but not appropriate. The prospects we discard while digging reflect our desire to only pursue those whose needs we can righteously meet, regardless of the toil it takes on our energy or emotions.

A righteous attitude while questioning is revealed when we sense what we're selling is not needed. It also shows when we persist in questioning to uncover genuine needs for what we sell. With serving others as a priority, we should question to uncover compelling reasons for continuing the sales process. Those reasons should never be directly related to personal glory or a potential paycheck.

During presentations, we demonstrate a righteous attitude toward serving others when we ask a prospect for feedback to ensure that we are presenting what's needed. Depending on the answer we receive, our next step will be to continue the presentation or stop the presentation to go back through the previous stages of the sales process, searching for more substantive needs.

In closing a sale, a righteous attitude compels us to complete the process ethically and correctly. As people selling righteously, our close should reinforce our commitment to serve clients honestly and compassionately without any attitudes born out of greed or self-serving ambitions.

With a righteous attitude, we use the truth about what we sell and how we sell it to overcome objections. This proves we want to serve others through faith in God and not through any personal plan for compensation or recognition. Those attitudes may cause us to overpromise, deceive, or manipulate our prospects and clients—practices we exclude from our sales process as people committed to selling God's way.

Righteous Instructions

The inherent authority in each sales situation can bring clarity about all aspects of the service needed. This axiom applies not only to sales but to any situation where a person serves. If someone wants to serve in a political party, the political leaders can tell them exactly who to vote for in each election. A coach can tell the players exactly how to perform to serve the team. The Bible contains precise instructions for those of us desiring to serve God. In the opening story of this chapter, Abraham had given Eliezer explicit instructions for finding a wife for his son.

During the sales process, we must extract specific service directives and expectations from all accessible authorities. This information is essential for selling God's way. If service instructions and expectations are not clear, then we need to approach all available authorities for clarity about what is needed and why. The authorities are the people who can say yes or no to buying what we sell. However, we should heed the service instructions from anyone in a client's organization. Those without authority to say yes or no can influence the perception of our service by communicating what they experienced while interacting with us.

Of course, just as important as securing the service instructions and expectations is the execution of those edicts. If what we are asked to do aligns with Christian principles, then we must provide the service desired.

Extract Instructions

During the sales process, we must extract specific service directives and expectations from all accessible authorities. This information is essential to selling God's way.

Righteous Responses

The book of Ephesians says we should serve wholeheartedly as if we're serving the Lord and not people. In this chapter's story of exemplary service, Rebekah called Eliezer "Lord" and then quickly responded to his request for water. The principle put forth in Ephesians, along with the example set by Rebekah, requires righteous salespeople to adopt an attitude that makes us rapidly respond to any request with a reverent desire to serve, as if God almighty, the Creator of the universe, made a request, knowing that if He asked for something, we'd use whatever resources we had available to get it immediately (see Ephesians 6:7).

While selling advertising, I would get requests for tickets, trips, toys, and talent appearances. My responsibility was to fulfill each request quickly with whatever resources I had at hand. If I didn't have what was requested, then I had to quickly inform the client and suggest alternatives.

Respond Righteously

Rapidly respond to any request with a reverent desire to serve.

Righteous Anticipation

Embracing an attitude that anticipates future needs is a three-stage sequence. First, it motivates us to prepare before the selling begins in anticipation of the needs to come. This calls for us to organize, at the very least, the basics of what we offer in an excellent manner. In the story above, Rebekah came out to the spring with a jar on her shoulder in anticipation of gathering water to serve others.

Before the selling began at any radio station, the company needed to secure a significant number of listeners in a format favorable for marketing messages. This motivation to construct a viable radio format with a responsive audience came from anticipating a client's advertising needs.

Second, an attitude that anticipates prompts us to perceive, predict, and please regarding any needs that occur while selling. Rebekah observed the camels while serving Eliezer and then acted righteously in presuming and satisfying their thirst.

While selling advertising, I often observed prospects needing more education regarding advertising to be properly served by and the radio station and me. In those instances, I would enlighten rather than sell because the prospect needed a better understanding of the different advertising philosophies and principles before investing in any radio station.

Third, adopting an attitude that anticipates inspires us to deliver satisfactory service after the selling ends. This often requires us to add more assets to the initial services offered during our presentation. In this chapter's service story, we see Eliezer serving by not only finding a wife for Abraham's son but also praying for success in finding a wife with a servant's heart, asking God to verify the woman's heart for service through her behavior at the spring. In this way, he would deliver a wife capable of satisfying the future needs of his master's family, long after he had completed the assignment given to him.

Discussing the exact results a client expected from their advertising enabled me to meet needs, long after their commercials stopped airing on the radio station. I accomplished this by adding assets to the services offered during the initial presentation. I would add more commercials to a campaign, perhaps change the commercial's marketing message, or include sponsorship of an event. My righteous anticipation of needs motivated me to revise services to ensure the client remained satisfied, long after the advertising ended.

Anticipate Needs

Embracing an attitude that anticipates future needs is a three-stage sequence. First, it motivates us to prepare before the selling begins. Second, it prompts us to perceive, predict, and please regarding any needs that may occur while selling. Finally, it inspires us to deliver satisfactory service after the selling ends.

Righteous Plan

In Eliezer's quest to succeed, he journeyed with ten camels and various valuables given to him by Abraham. Eliezer used these things to successfully find a wife for Abraham's son and to persuade her to follow him. After Rebekah finished serving Eliezer and the camels, he put a gold ring in her nose and two gold bracelets on her arm. It's clear to see that Eliezer planned to serve by using the most valuable resources at his disposal.

Our quest to succeed at selling means having a plan for delivering superior customer service. Our plan should make use of available assets and people power in a manner that provides all we need to deliver the best possible service in a gracious and glorious manner. We are to serve as if we were working for the Lord, not people.

Prepare Thoroughly

Our plan must prepare us to deliver superior service in a gracious and glorious manner by equipping ourselves with all available assets and people power.

In selling everything from eggs to advertising, I experienced noteworthy success whenever I entered a sales process armed with the best possible resources. Of course, this required my grandfather and the companies I worked for to plan and organize themselves around their best possible assets. My grandfather did this by selling fresh eggs that were laid locally. Soon after the eggs were laid, my grandfather would prepare them to be sold at a price lower than the grocery store, even though they were fresher than the eggs sold at the grocery store. The most successful radio stations I worked for used their resources to secure the most talented people and best technical assets, using nondiscriminatory hiring practices and surveys to ascertain what the audience, advertisers, and employees expected from an excellent radio station.

My grandfather and these radio stations succeeded because they possessed a righteous plan that gave priority to serving people and not just earning profits. Logically, the opposite is true: If an organization makes plans for profits without giving priority to the people being served, it fails, most likely because of inadequate resources and incompetent personnel. One radio station I worked for was never thoroughly prepared to use their available assets or people power to serve others. The station's management consistently made decisions without any passion to serve employees, advertisers, or an audience. Consequentially, this station consistently dealt with the defection of employees and advertisers, dwindling audience, and declining revenue.

Righteous Passions

In the book of Colossians, the Apostle Paul instructs believers to work as if we are working for the Lord because it is Jesus Christ we're serving. Imagine if the Lord hired us to sell something to serve Christ. This would lift us to an unparalleled level of excitement. Our fervor for serving would be at its highest point. Before we even started selling, our passion to succeed would motivate us to gain a complete understanding of our product and potential customers. While selling, we would work diligently to behave superbly. After the selling ended, we would ensure customer satisfaction became and remained superior (see Colossians 3:23–24).

Our selling behavior needs to embody the same attitude I just described. This generates a passion that allows us to serve righteously, while giving us a standard for assessing our situation and adjusting our attitudes. Eliezer is an excellent example of someone analyzing their situation and adopting an attitude that reveals the passions of a faithful person. We see his concern that he might not be able to find a woman willing to journey with him back to Abraham's home, which means he would not be successful in serving his master. Then we see him in a passionate prayer requesting kindness, asking God to guide him so that he can successfully serve Abraham.

To help myself serve passionately, I mentally replaced the prospect I was attempting to serve with thought that I was striving to serve Jesus. This motivated me to go through a process where I analyzed everything, seeking to discover if what I was doing aligned with serving the Lord.

Analyze Everything

In the book of Colossians, the Apostle Paul instructs believers to work as if we're working for the Lord because it's ultimately Jesus Christ we're serving. This principle should motivate us to analyze our selling and service efforts to discover whether what we're doing aligns with the actions of a person serving the Lord.

Righteous Effort

When we serve righteously, we use our most important asset, faith, to please God and serve others. According to the Bible, faith is being sure of what we hope for and certain of what we do not see. Serving faithfully means we work diligently to experience the goodness of God, even when the goodness we hope for remains unseen or undetected. It also means we remain certain that the blessings that come from trusting God will unquestionably arrive. The goodness that most salespeople hope for includes things like money, positions, or possessions related to society's definition of success. However, the blessings we receive as people selling God's way can include those things, along with far more important valuables, such as grace, mercy, purpose, wisdom, peace, love, and righteous character growth (see Hebrews 11:1).

In Eliezer and Rebekah's story, both people behaved in ways that demonstrated their faith in God. Eliezer prayed to God for success, and Rebekah upon hearing about Eliezer's prayer, instantly agreed to follow him (see Genesis 24:56–58).

Serve Faithfully

Serving faithfully means we work diligently to experience the goodness of God, even though the goodness we hope for remains unseen or undetected. It also means we remain certain that the blessings that come from trusting God will unquestionably arrive.

Great Sellers Are Great Servers

The desire to achieve greatness lies within everyone. What differs among us is the path we take to become great. Some work to achieve greatness strictly using their intellect and work ethic, while others seek greatness on a path to attain popularity or a position. These skills and motivations in themselves are not evil if used righteously. In fact, if we achieve greatness righteously, some of these things may be the reason for our success. However, faith is the core component of any approach we take to achieve success as people selling God's way. It leads us to trust in God and His principles to serve others and achieve success, knowing that even greatness is achievable when we follow the teachings of Jesus Christ and serve others. What Jesus says about greatness can be found in the Gospel of Matthew, where He declares that whoever wants to be great must be a servant.

So, if we want to be great at selling, we must be great at serving, knowing that our level of success lies not in the number of people we sell to, but in the number of people we serve—the people whose needs we righteously meet as we prioritize pleasing God and loving others over any personal plans or pain (see Matthew 20:26).

The truth about our greatness as salespeople can be calculated through the number of clients we righteously serve—clients who consistently express their satisfaction through repeated contracts, strong recommendations, and brand loyal conduct. When those numbers decline or stagnate, it may be a sign that our greatness is decreasing, and failure is on the horizon.

Success and Service

Our success lies not in the number of people we correctly sell to, but in the number of people we righteously serve.

Questions

1. What is your current way to measure customer satisfaction? Does it factor in repeat contracts or referrals?

2. What are your service goals at work?

3. What is more important to you while selling: serving customers or earning an income? Why?

4. What do you think Jesus meant when He said greatness is related to service?

5. Identify three things that you could do to serve your customers better. Would your customers identify these same three things? What would your customers say are the top three things that you could do to provide better customer service?

Scriptural References

- Throughout all history, the best example of service will forever be Jesus, who said that He came to serve and not to be served:

  "*For even the Son of Man did not come to be served, but to serve, and to give his life as a ransom for many*" (Mark 10:45).

- We should serve wholeheartedly by responding rapidly to a request, as if we are serving God and not a person:

  Serve wholeheartedly, as if you were serving the Lord, not people (Ephesians 6:7).

- We should work at selling with all our heart, as if God and not a person hired us:

  Whatever you do, work at it with all your heart, as working for the Lord, not for human masters, since you know that you will receive an inheritance from the Lord as a reward. It is the Lord Christ you are serving (Colossians 3:23–24).

- Working faithfully to serve means we labor diligently to experience the goodness of God, even when the goodness we hope for remains unseen or undetectable. It also means we remain certain that the blessings that come from trusting God unquestionably arrive:

  Now faith is confidence in what we hope for and assurance about what we do not see (Hebrews 11:1).

- Rebekah's faith was demonstrated when she heard Eliezer's prayer and then instantly agreed to follow him:

  But he said to them, "Do not detain me, now that the Lord has granted success to my journey. Send me on my way so I may go to my master." Then they said, "Let's call the young woman and ask her about it." So they called Rebekah and asked her, "Will you go with this man?" "I will go," she said (Genesis 24:56–58).

- The truth about our greatness as salespeople can be calculated by the number of people we righteously serve, not the number of people we sell to:

  Not so with you. Instead, whoever wants to become great among you must be your servant (Matthew 20:26).

CHAPTER 11:

What Not to Do

Therefore, I urge you, brothers and sisters, in view of God's mercy, to offer your bodies as a living sacrifice, holy and pleasing to God—this is your true and proper worship. Do not conform to the pattern of this world, but be transformed by the renewing of your mind. Then you will be able to test and approve what God's will is—his good, pleasing and perfect will.

For by the grace given me I say to every one of you: Do not think of yourself more highly than you ought, but rather think of yourself with sober judgment, in accordance with the faith God has distributed to each of you. For just as each of us has one body with many members, and these members do not all have the same function, so in Christ we though many form one body, and each member belongs to all the others. We have different gifts, according to the grace given us. If your gift is prophesying, then prophesy in accordance with your

> *faith; if it is serving, then serve; if it is teaching, then teach; if it is to encourage, then give encouragement; if it is giving, then give generously; if it is to lead, do it diligently; if it is to show mercy, do it cheerfully.*
>
> —Romans 12:1–8

Do not Conform to Worldly Patterns

In AD 57, the Apostle Paul sent instructions to Roman Christians that are still valuable for believers today. In his directions, Paul discussed what to believe and how to behave. One of the most important things he said is that in view of God's mercy, while living in these bodies, we should make sacrifices. This means we should give up things, establish boundaries, avoid certain behaviors, and not satisfy every desire. Some biblical translations call this "*our reasonable act of service.*"

These sacrifices can be seen as reasonable because in sending His only Son to die for our sins, God extended us great mercy. We need this mercy because none of us are completely righteous. We've all sinned and fallen short of God's standards, time after time. After death, we deserve damnation, doomed to an eternal life in hell where there is weeping and gnashing of teeth. However, Jesus saved us from this fate. As believers in Jesus as Lord and Savior, we will have eternal life in Heaven after death. As faithful followers of Jesus Christ, we will spend eternity with God in paradise. Jesus's sacrificial death paved the way for this reconciliation with God and released us from our sin debt (see Matthew 13:49–50, Romans 3:10, and Romans 5:10–11).

Therefore, we should make the appropriate sacrifices to sell righteously. We do this through using our God-given spiritual gifts and natural talents, while not thinking more highly of ourselves than we ought. We sacrifice while selling when we do not conform to worldly ways of conducting business. Using worldly ways in selling expresses a desire for sinful pleasures, a conviction to satisfy some sort of lust, and a preoccupation with our own selfish desires. However, making sacrifices and selling God's way expresses a spiritual act of worship, which is holy and pleasing to God. It is also supremely beneficial to our customers (see 1 John 2:15–17).

Do Not Conform to Any Worldly Patterns of Selling

Most salespeople follow a worldly pattern when they decide to sell for self-serving ambitions related to money and status, rather being motivated by ethics and responsibility to serve other people. Salespeople who are not selling righteously hunt for buyers instead of seeking to find appropriate prospects; thus, they settle for prospects who marginally match the type of potential buyer needed. Most often, an insincere period of questioning follows. Salespeople stuck in worldly ways of selling ask questions designed to manipulate rather than uncover needs. What's likely to happen next is that they deliver a presentation filled with over-inflated prices, deceitful declarations, and incomplete comparisons, followed by a close and handling of objections that are inconsiderate and self-serving. Too often, their service turns out to be dissatisfying, sometimes leaving a client in debt and discouraged. Obviously, there are numerous ways a person could incorporate unrighteousness into a sales process. But all selling sins have the potential to not only ruin relationships and reputations, but also economies and communities.

As I write this book, much of the world walks around in an economic nightmare, brought about by corrupt and evil selling practices born out of greed, fears, and self-serving ambitions. Home buying and selling suffer severely because of the high prices of housing and mortgage companies selling financing to people who only marginally fit the criteria of a prospective buyer. Auto sales continually remain inconsistent because of consumer distrust and self-serving sales practices. Most car companies have issued fearful forecasts about their future as most people dread buying a car because they anticipate dealing with a dishonest salesperson. The financial markets make news because of the millions of dollars lost by greedy self-serving executives who used manipulated research, deceitful accounting practices, and false reasoning to sell their services and explain their enormous bonuses. Pharmaceutical companies flood doctors' offices with salespeople motivated to sell more medicine regardless of patient needs. Energy companies, whose profits reach into the billions, function with an ever-increasing pricing scale, lobbying effort, and advertising budget—for the apparent purpose of selling governments and the public an inaccurate picture of their plight and plans.

Most companies operate with the belief that sales, revenue, and profits need to increase continually, even though their market may contain a decreasing number of customers. Most often, because of a company or entire industry treating their buyers sinfully. Unrighteous selling and marketing practices decrease the number of potential customers in the marketplace.

Many companies do unscrupulous things to their own salespeople. Sellers have been hired under false pretenses to work toward incomes and promotions that are improbable or not even possible. Too many sellers' results have been judged inaccurately because their manager chose standards based upon unsound premises and faulty assumptions. For instance, they may assume all territories or account lists have the same revenue potential, or they may assume a certain salesperson does not possess the technical acumen, attention to detail, or skillset needed to succeed in a particular sales position—even though this salesperson never received adequate training. Such demoralizing treatment within companies leaves salespeople with poor or unacceptable results, which often leads to discouragement, poor performance reviews, and loss of employment.

We need people and companies selling with a renewed mindset, developing revenue goals around accurate assessments and service-driven ambitions. This begins by relating success to how many customers get *served* as opposed to how many get *sold;* the process should continue with abandoning any previous pattern of conducting business or treating people unrighteously.

Selling Sins

The selling sins summarized in this book have the potential to ruin not only relationships and reputations but also economies and communities.

Do Not Underestimate the Power to Be Transformed by Renewing Your Mind

We need to change, no longer selling in ways that accommodate greed, deceit, fear, or self-serving ambitions. Far too many careers, customers, and companies have suffered because of unrighteous selling behavior. To make this transition from sellers behaving sinfully to people selling God's way, we need to renew our minds. Renewing our minds means renovating our thought process and emotional framework. It means taking out old things such as the priority given to profits and putting in new things such as priority given to service. In our renovating, we need to tear down that wall of fear that prevents us from walking away from prospects who are suspects. As we open the door of faith that leads us to pray for appropriate prospects, we need to raise the bar in communicating so that we can build in areas of truth and transparency. In our transformation, we must take out the mirrors that motivate us to reflect an image that society deems successful and install mirrors that lead us to emulate Jesus. If we have become accustomed to closing sales and handling objections with greed and deceit, we must cease using that approach and learn to close sales with humility and honesty.

Renewing our minds righteously, means seeing things from Jesus's perspective, a view that allows us to uncover and verify the specifics of God's will for our life. The book of Jeremiah says that God has plans to prosper and not to harm us, plans to give us a hope and a future. By renovating our minds with godly things, we will find and maintain peace, goodness, and satisfaction while selling. The Bible tells us that God's will for our lives is perfect, pleasing, and superior (see Jeremiah 9:11 and Romans 12:2).

Economic Nightmare

As I write this book, much of the world walks around in an economic nightmare brought about by corrupt and evil selling practices, born out of greed, fears, and self-serving ambitions.

Do Not Think of Yourself More Highly Than You Ought

Thinking of ourselves more highly than we ought leads to an attitude of entitlement, driving us to seek self-serving gratifications, rather than seeking opportunities to serve. Self-serving thinking motivates us to meet our own needs ahead of the needs of others. It is also counterproductive for anyone seeking referrals, recommendations, and repeat customers because the priority becomes self-satisfaction and not customer satisfaction. To maximize your income and business relationships, you need a steady flow of well-satisfied, righteously served, customers, who express that satisfaction through referrals, recommendations, and repeat contracts. If you have past customers who refuse to refer others to you, post negative reviews, or decline to buy from you again, your capacity for greatness in sales will be severely crippled. As I stated in chapter 10, our greatness as salespeople depends not in the number of people we sell to, but in the number of people we righteously serve.

Thinking of ourselves too highly opens a door to the perilous pit of pride, which can overpower our decision-making process. We start relying on other sources besides God's Word for wisdom and rewards. Our intellect and intuition become the final authority as to what we will do or say while selling, or we apply advice from people whose knowledge we deem better than God's. This most often leaves us in opposition to God, void of the grace needed to succeed during our own mistakes. The Bible says that God opposes the proud but gives grace to the humble (see James 4:6).

Instead of thinking highly of ourselves, we need to think of ourselves in the manner found in this chapter's opening Scripture (Romans 12:1–8). This starts by humbly accepting the fact that as people of faith, we form one body through Christ. As members of the body of Christian believers, we each hold a place that makes the entire body productive and valuable. We each have a responsibility to all the past, present, and future members. No one member is more valuable or important than another because we all need each other to succeed.

Each one of us needs to fulfill the responsibilities that come with our position. That responsibility inspires us to willingly treat each prospect and customer with a servant's heart that is filled with grace, truth, and love. We want our customers to be successful and flourish in part because of what we just sold them, as we righteously interacted with them. It is impossible to be a successful salesperson without successful clients, just like it is impossible to be a successful teacher or doctor, without successful students and patients.

We must never forget that our talents and spiritual gifts come from God. We are born with innate talents, aptitudes and capabilities demonstrated from birth. Then we receive spiritual gifts, after we receive Jesus Christ as Lord and Savior. Now we must nurture and maximize these gifts and talents to righteously excel at all aspects of living, which obviously include selling righteously for those who choose a sales profession. We should never use our spiritual gifts and natural talents to satisfy sinful desires. Our godly resources should help us to overcome temptations, not surrender to them. Satisfying sinful desires and surrendering to inappropriate temptations while selling abuses people and resources. It leads us down a path that damages revenue and relationships—especially our fellowship with God and our bond with customers, who are the exact people we need to succeed.

Ruining Revenue and Relationships

Our godly resources should help us to overcome temptations, not to surrender to them. Satisfying sinful desires and surrendering to inappropriate temptations while selling abuses people and resources, damaging revenue and relationships.

Do Not Surrender to Temptations

The Bible describes Satan as a tempter and states that we are also tempted by our own evil desires. Through the combination of Satan's schemes and our own evil desires, people everywhere are tempted to sin. Consequently, as salespeople, we will be tempted to do unrighteous things while selling; there are no exceptions. These temptations will invite us to omit or distort information and imply guarantees that are not likely to occur. These temptations may also urge us to manipulate numbers and prices to our clients and bosses. Not mentioned in these temptations, which are invitations to sin include dissatisfied customers, damaged relationships, and loss of future sales that occur if a salesperson's unrighteous acts become known. These invitations to sin will be delivered in a desirable package to make more money, obtain a better position, or avoid losing a sale. If we surrender to these temptations, we will do so disregarding biblical principles, in exchange for temporary gratifications.

These temptations often arrive when we are in the midst overcoming a trial or becoming righteously successful. During these times, we can find ourselves faced with what we may see as an opportunity to take the shortest route to success. However, if we analyze these opportunities righteously, we will see these temptations as invitations to sin. But God is faithful. So, when temptations arrive, we should find and follow the righteous path that God always provides. For salespeople, this means we find a way to make sales along a path that includes integrity, love, and service.

The Bible reminds us to consider Jesus, so we do not grow weary and lose heart during our struggles. Jesus did not give in and abandon doing God's will in exchange for self-centered needs. Jesus suffered and bled so we can obtain a new life empowered by God's Holy Spirit. He continued to love and serve each one of us as He suffered overwhelming agony. Let us not forget the model Jesus exemplified whenever we resist temptations to sin and strive to sell in a loving and service-minded manner. Through the Holy Spirit, we can overcome any invitation, or temptation to sin, regardless of its intensity or duration. It is doubtful that any of us will ever have to bear being beaten and nailed to a cross, as we resist the temptation to sin. (see Hebrews 12:3–4).

Do Not Pursue Greatness Without Jesus Christ

The desire for greatness while selling is not sinful. Seeking to build a successful sales career is not an evil desire. These desires become evil when we try to accomplish success through habitually incorporating sinful activities. There are explicit commandments and teachings in the Bible against lying, stealing, deceiving, coveting, greed, and self-serving ambitions.

We sin whenever we exaggerate or conceal facts. We sin if we manipulate research or turn opinions into facts. We sin by coveting a position or status so much that it motivates us to mistreat a coworker. We sin in serving up whatever a person wants to hear, instead of speaking truthfully. As sellers, we sin whenever we exaggerate benefits, understate risk, manipulate research, misrepresent services, mismanage expectations, or present unfair prices. Listing all the sinful activities of sellers would be extensive and exhaustive.

However, whenever we sin, death most definitely occurs. The Bible says that the wages of sin are death, but the gift of God is eternal life in Jesus Christ. The type of life or death is relative. Sinning may not cause a physical death. But we may experience the death of a sale, career, or relationship. The "life" could be a buyer becoming active or the acquisition of a sales skill that lasts a lifetime (see Romans 6:23 and James 1:13–15).

As people selling righteously, we have much more at stake than just the death of a sale. We have at risk our walk with God, our fellowship with the almighty Creator. We should always want to stay connected to God, as we embrace Christ-centered living, because Scripture tells us that through Jesus, all our needs are met. This calls for us to faithfully believe that through remaining in Jesus and Him remaining in us, we will bear much fruit. We also believe that without Jesus, nothing worthwhile can be accomplished. I covered this concept extensively in chapter 2.

Evil Desires

The desire for greatness while selling is not evil. Seeking to build a successful sales career is not an evil desire. These desires become evil when we try to accomplish them through habitually incorporating sinful activities. There are explicit commandments and teachings in the Bible against lying, stealing, deceiving, coveting, greed, and self-serving ambitions.

Do Not Let the Devil Destroy Your Faith

Satan wants to destroy our faith. Through faith, we formed our relationship with God. In this relationship, we not only become members of God's army fighting against Satan, but we also lead others to do so. When we sell God's way, we put our faith into action. We say to Satan and the entire world that we believe in God, Jesus, and the Holy Spirit. We take a bold stance that demonstrates our belief in the inerrancy of the Bible and the power of prayer. We also encourage others to believe in God and do things His way.

As people selling righteously, we are striving to maximize our take-home pay, build the best possible business relationships, and devoutly live a Christ-centered life. We want God's will to be accomplished in our lives and throughout the entire planet, just as it is in heaven. This also demonstrates our trust in Jesus to deliver blessings in abundance and eternal life. Selling God's way makes us enemies of the devil. We have in effect attacked the satanic world by faithfully showing our love for God and other people while selling. We need to remain alert because the devil can be a relentless enemy. Jesus says that Satan comes to steal, kill, and destroy (see John 10:10).

Since the beginning, Satan has tempted people (Adam and Eve) to disobey and go against God's will. Satan wants us to forsake God. He seeks to deceive us into not believing or trusting God. This can destroy our purpose for living and steal our earthly success. The devil desires to decrease the number of people who do things God's way.

First Peter chapter 5 says that the devil prowls around looking for someone to devour and that we should resist him by standing firm in faith, knowing that Christians everywhere suffer the same kind of fate. Jesus also says Satan was a murderer from the beginning and a liar—in fact, the father of all lies (see John 8:44 and 1 Peter 5:7–9).

Deceives and Destroys

The devil seeks to deceive us into not believing or trusting God. This can destroy our purpose for living and steal our earthly success. Since the beginning, Satan has tempted and lied to people (Adam and Eve) to get them to go against God's will.

Do Not Accept the Mark on Your Head or Hand

The book of Revelation says the day will come when a beast who is much like a person will try to force everyone to receive a mark on their hand or forehead. This mark authorizes a person to buy or sell. The name of the beast, or the number associated with his name, is the mark. Right now, as I write this book, much is unknown. But his number is 666. As faithful followers of Jesus Christ, selling God's way, we must not accept this mark on our body.

More specifics regarding this terrible time will become known as this age approaches. However, we do know that during this time, people devoted to Jesus Christ are beheaded because they do not accept the mark, worship the beast, or revere his image. Those who worship the beast, revere his image, or receive the mark that allows them to buy, or sell, will suffer a fate far worse than the beheaded followers of Jesus. The beheaded followers of Jesus Christ who have not worshipped the beast, revered his image, or accepted the mark that allows them to buy or sell, will rise again, reigning with Jesus for a thousand years, and dwell eternally in heaven. The concluding verses in the Bible that illuminate this era state that "*this means that God's holy people must endure persecutions patiently, always obey God's commands, and maintain their faith in Jesus*" (see Revelation 14:9–12 and Revelation 20:4–5).

Do Not Forget We Are Ambassadors of Jesus Christ

The Apostle Paul says we are ambassadors of Christ. An ambassador is a kingdom's official representative, working diplomatically in a foreign land. In the context of selling, the foreign land we work in is the business world. There, we represent the kingdom of God. It's our responsibility to interact with everyone in a manner that shows our kingdom stands for love, service, and righteousness, regardless of circumstances (see 2 Corinthians 5:20).

We must never forget that as ambassadors of Jesus Christ, we can lead others to sell God's way. Other businesspeople will be watching us, interpreting our behavior as either righteous or unrighteous. This gives us the opportunity to set an example that leads others to do things righteously—God's way (see 1 Timothy 4:12).

Exercising the following three principles will help greatly as we interact with others in the business world. These three principles can help us not to conform to any worldly patterns of selling but to be transformed by the renewing of our minds. These principles can help in our personal battles to resist temptations and thrive. As ambassadors of Christ, our goal is to serve as shining examples and genuine representations of people being blessed through selling righteously.

- *Believe God Is Faithful*: The first principle requires us to wholeheartedly believe and rely on the fact that God is faithful. As a faithful God, He will be there to direct, protect, and correct us through every trial, tragedy, and temptation. His Holy Spirit dwells in us and with every temptation, God provides a way of escape, so we don't have to surrender to evil desires or satanic schemes. Furthermore, every temptation that comes is common to all other people as well. Salespeople everywhere will battle the same types of temptations to stray from selling righteously that we face. Our struggles do not shock God or catch Him unprepared; He will help you and countless others turn evil into good. Nothing exists that God cannot conquer or control (see 1 Corinthians 10:13).
- *Fasten a Firm Hold to the Faith We Profess*: The second principle calls for us to fasten a firm hold onto the faith we profess. Jesus was tempted in every way, just like us, yet He remained sin-free. Therefore, He can sympathize with our weaknesses as we come to God requesting resolutions, restorations, and provisions. We will need His help because none of us is able to always sell perfectly righteously. So, we will need God's love, grace, and mercy to be blessed and sanctified while selling righteously. Jesus makes it possible for us to approach God's throne of grace with confidence, knowing it is there we find much-needed mercy. "Grace" may be defined by the acrostic: "God's Riches At Christ's Expense." Mercy can be defined as freedom from a deserved punishment or self-caused pain (see Hebrews 2:18 and Hebrews 4:14–16).

- *Remain Watchful and Pray*: The third principle encourages us to remain watchful and pray, because even though our spirits are willing, our bodies can be weak. Therefore, we remain susceptible to temptations, illnesses, and the evil desires of our flesh. The temptation to stray from selling righteously will pop up when we least expect it. We fight off this weakness by being alert and seeking God's guidance. Being aware of our own evil desires, emotions, and Satan's schemes is a significant step toward avoiding and absorbing unrighteous thoughts and behavior. It also puts us on our knees, praying for God's direction, correction, and protection (see Matthew 26:41).

Questions

1. What are some consequences of not selling God's way or disregarding the Word of God while selling?

2. If all things are possible through God, how does that influence the way you sell?

3. Are there things you will not do to make a sale? Why? Are you ever tempted to do things you know are violations of God's commands while selling?

4. How do you handle temptations that occur as you sell?

5. How would you sell if money and income were not a driving motivation?

Scriptural References

- Due to sin and unrighteousness, some are doomed to spend eternity in a fiery furnace:

  This is how it will be at the end of the age. The angels will come and separate the wicked from the righteous and throw them into the fiery furnace, where there will be weeping and gnashing of teeth (Matthew 13:49–50).

  We *all* qualify for this fate because none of us is completely righteous:

  As it is written: "There is no one righteous, not even one" (Romans 3:10).

- Jesus's sacrifice on the cross gave us the way to be reconciled with God and released from our sin debt:

  For if, when we were God's enemies, we were reconciled to him through the death of his Son, how much more, having been reconciled, shall we be saved through his life! Not only is this so, but we also rejoice in God through our Lord Jesus Christ, through whom we have now received reconciliation (Romans 5:10–11).

- Conducting business using worldly ways expresses a desire for sinful pleasures, a motivation to satisfy lust, and a preoccupation with oneself:

  Do not love the world or anything in the world. If anyone loves the world, love for the Father is not in them. For everything in the world—the lust of the flesh, the lust of the eyes, and the pride of life—comes not from the Father but from the world. The world and its desires pass away, but whoever does the will of God lives forever (1 John 2:15–17).

- God's plans for our lives are great. Let us embrace doing things His way.

  For I know the plans I have for you, declares the L*ORD*, *"plans to prosper you and not to harm you, plans to give you hope and a future"* (Jeremiah 29:11).

- God's will for our lives is perfect, pleasing, and superior:

  Do not conform to the pattern of this world, but be transformed by the renewing of your mind. Then you will be able to test and approve what God's will is—his good, pleasing and perfect will (Romans 12:2).

- Pride puts us in opposition to God, void of the grace needed to succeed in the midst of our own mistakes:

  But he gives us more grace. That is why Scripture says: "God opposes the proud but gives grace to the humble" (James 4:6).

- Resist the temptation to sin by considering Jesus:

  Consider him who endured such opposition from sinners, so that you will not grow weary and lose heart. In your struggle against sin, you have not yet resisted to the point of shedding your blood (Hebrews 12:3–4).

- Sin results in death, but the gift of God brings eternal life. Death could be the end of a sales career or relationship. Life could be a prospect becoming a buyer or the acquisition of a sales skill that lasts a lifetime:

  For the wages of sin is death, but the gift of God is eternal life in Christ Jesus our Lord (Romans 6:23).

- Some temptations arise out of our own evil desires:

  When tempted, no one should say, "God is tempting me." For God cannot be tempted by evil, nor does he tempt anyone; but each one is tempted when they are dragged away by their own evil desire and enticed. Then, after desire has conceived, it gives birth to sin; and sin, when it is full-grown, gives birth to death (James 1:13–15).

- Satan seeks to destroy our faith:

  The thief comes only to steal and kill and destroy; I have come that they may have life, and have it to the full (John 10:10).

- Satan seeks to deceive us into not believing or trusting God, destroying our purpose for living and stealing our earthly success:

  You belong to your father, the devil, and you want to carry out your father's desire. He was a murderer from the beginning, not holding to the truth, for there is no truth in him. When he lies, he speaks his native language, for he is a liar and the father of lies (John 8:44).

- Jesus cares for us. The devil desires to devour us:

  Cast all your anxiety on him because he cares for you. Be alert and of sober mind. Your enemy the devil prowls around like a roaring lion looking for someone to devour. Resist him, standing firm in the faith, because you know that the family of believers throughout the world is undergoing the same kind of sufferings (1 Peter 5:7–9).

- Those who worship the beast, revere his image, or accept the mark on their hand or head will experience God's fury and full wrath, eventually suffering eternity in hell:

  A third angel followed them and said in a loud voice: "If anyone worships the beast and its image and receives its mark on their forehead or on their hand, they, too, will drink the wine of God's fury, which has been poured full strength into the cup of his wrath. They will be tormented with burning sulfur in the presence of the holy angels and of the Lamb. And the smoke of their torment will rise for ever and ever. There will be no rest day or night for those who worship the beast and its image, or for anyone who receives the mark of its name." This calls for patient endurance on the part of the people of God who keep his commands and remain faithful to Jesus (Revelation 14:9–12).

- The beheaded followers of Jesus Christ who have not worshipped the beast, revered his image, or accepted the mark that allows them to buy or sell, will rise again, reigning with Jesus for a thousand years, and dwelling eternally in Heaven:

  I saw thrones on which were seated those who had been given authority to judge. And I saw the souls of those who had been beheaded because of their testimony about Jesus and because of the word of God. They had not worshiped the beast or its image and had not received its mark on their foreheads or their hands. They came to life and reigned with Christ a thousand years. (The rest of the dead did not come to life until the thousand years were ended.) This is the first resurrection (Revelation 20:4–5).

- We are ambassadors of Jesus Christ:

  We are therefore Christ's ambassadors, as though God were making his appeal through us. We implore you on Christ's behalf: Be reconciled to God (2 Corinthians 5:20).

- Selling righteously gives us the opportunity to set an example that leads others to do things righteously—God's way:

  Don't let anyone look down on you because you are young, but set an example for the believers in speech, in conduct, in love, in faith and in purity (1 Timothy 4:12).

- God will not let us be tempted with more than we can tolerate:

  No temptation has overtaken you except what is common to mankind. And God is faithful; he will not let you be tempted beyond what you can bear. But when you are tempted, he will also provide a way out so that you can endure it (1 Corinthians 10:13).

- Jesus suffered through the same kinds of temptations that we experience. He can empathize, sympathize, and help us during our struggles:

  Because he himself suffered when he was tempted, he is able to help those who are being tempted (Hebrews 2:18).

- Jesus understands our weaknesses; this makes it possible for us to approach the throne of grace with confidence:

  Therefore, since we have a great high priest who ascended into heaven, Jesus the Son of God, let us hold firmly to the faith we profess. For we do not have a high priest who is unable to empathize with our weaknesses, but we have one who has been tempted in every way, just as we are—yet was without sin. Let us then approach the throne of grace with confidence, so that we may receive mercy and find grace to help us in our time of need (Hebrews 4:14–16).

- We fight off temptations by being alert and praying:

  Watch and pray so that you will not fall into temptation. The spirit is willing, but the body is weak (Matthew 26:41).

CHAPTER 12:

What to Do

Ask and it will be given to you; seek and you will find; knock and the door will be opened to you. For everyone who asks receives; he who seeks finds; and to the one who knocks, the door will be opened. Which of you, if your son asks for bread, will give him a stone? Or if he asks for a fish, will give him a snake? If you, then, though you are evil, know how to give good gifts to your children, how much more will your Father in heaven give good gifts to those who ask him! So in everything, do to others what you would have them do to you, for this sums up the Law and the Prophets. Enter through the narrow gate. For wide is the gate and broad is the road that leads to destruction, and many enter through it. But small is the gate and narrow the road that leads to life, and only a few find it.

—Matthew 7:7–14

Ask, Seek, and Knock

Ask. Seek. Knock. God extends a personal invitation to us all. He does not force any of us into a personal relationship with Him. In the Scripture above, Jesus says that if we ask for the things of God, then those things will be given to us. If we seek, we will find. If we knock, the door will be opened. We must always believe our Father in Heaven gives good gifts to anyone who asks. Selling God's way is something we must pursue, searching for the best and most righteous thing to do or say in every selling situation. One of the great things about God is that He gives believers the Holy Spirit to be our comforter and counselor; He equips and empowers us with His Holy Spirit so we can serve, sell, love, and live righteously. In the book of Luke, Jesus says God will give the Holy Spirit to those who ask (see Luke 11:11–13).

In John 14, Jesus spoke of the Holy Spirit as also being an advocate and teacher. Romans 8 says the Holy Spirit helps us when we are weak and intercedes—He prays for us. So, the more we can bring our mind, will, and emotions in alignment with what the Holy Spirit is doing for us, the more we'll experience the love, power, and wisdom of God operating in our lives. This is spiritual empowerment, and it brings our attitudes and actions in concert with God's will and word. As people attempting to sell righteously, we must seek ways to be spiritually empowered as a priority. Of course, we should not neglect our intellectual growth, emotional well-being, and physical health. But by embracing God's will and word, we facilitate our intellectual advancement, emotional fitness, and physical vitality because we are accessing the universe's ultimate source of power and love for direction, correction, and protection.

We should be on a life path that facilitates spiritual empowerment, hoping to transform our character to be more like Jesus and less like a person driven by self-serving ambitions and unrighteous motivations. Of course, we're human, so we may stray from the righteous path and follow other ideologies and instincts. But by diligently seeking spiritual empowerment, we'll be able to accomplish things we could never do on our own and attain unimaginable success and growth as a person and salesperson. The Apostle Paul writes in Ephesians 3 that God can do immeasurably more than we can ask or imagine through His power at work in us. Yes, we can attain unimaginable blessings and guidance, even while selling, but we must ask God for them and diligently seek them (see John 14:26, Romans 8:26, and Ephesians 3:20).

Due to satanic schemes, sinful worldly ways, and our own evil desires, we're constantly bombarded with information and temptations that can lead us to live and sell in ways that are contrary to God's ways and spiritual empowerment. In Matthew 7:13–14, Jesus says that the gate is wide, and the road is broad that leads to destruction. Tragically, far too many salespeople find that wide gate and journey down that broad road by selling in ways that incorporate sin and self-serving ambitions. Jesus also says that the gate is small, and the road is narrow that leads to life, and only a few find it. Hopefully, the insights this book imparts will help you find that small gate so that you can journey up that narrow road (see Ephesians 5:5).

The seven steps that follow are designed to take you along a path of spiritual growth and guidance as you seek to sell righteously. There are many other things you can do to be empowered spiritually, such as being an active church member and reading books about Christian living, but these seven steps will help you apply the wisdom of God to your work life.

Seven Steps to Selling Righteously

Be Devoted to God

God must lord over our entire lives, not just over the things we do on Sundays and holidays. We must not compartmentalize our lives, only seeking God for weddings, funerals, and times of trouble. Our faith must be in God. The Bible says that "*without faith, it is impossible to please God because anyone who comes to him must believe that he exists and rewards those who earnestly seek him*" (Hebrews 11:6). This starts by believing God alone is sovereign. Our overriding aspiration must be to build our life around God's desires, trying our best to view everything from God's perspective, as we strive to serve and please Him in all that we do (see Exodus 20:1–3).

Jesus must be our Lord and Savior. We must rely on Him not only for salvation but also for instructions on how to live and grow spiritually. We must strive to be more like Jesus in the way we think and behave. Jesus says no one can serve two masters: either he will hate one and love the other, or he will be devoted to one and despise the other. He emphasizes we cannot serve both God and money. As people attempting to sell righteously, we must constantly ask ourselves whether what we're doing and saying reflects Christ-centered living, or our own desire to acquire more money (see Matthew 6:24).

Hopefully, salespeople realize that if they sell righteously, they'll reap the rewards sought through secular selling because selling God's way allows for the best possible relationships, as it maximizes take-home pay. One of the great things about God is that if we draw closer to Him, He will draw closer to us. If we humble ourselves, surrendering all areas of our life to His will and word, He will lift us up (see James 4:8–10).

Maximizing Revenue and Relationships

As salespeople, we can serve everyone greatly by selling God's way, which is the best way to maximize revenue and relationships.

Be a Doer of the Word and Not Just a Hearer

The entire premise for selling righteously rests on this principle, faithfully believing that God gives us everlasting guidance for everything through the Bible. Our challenge lies in applying God's Word to each second of living, especially when temptations and trials entice us to follow other ideologies and instincts instead of God's instructions. James implores us to continually read, hear, and study the perfect freedom given by God's Word, promising that anyone who never forgets the Word but obediently applies it to all aspects of living will be blessed (see James 1:22–25).

Obey Biblical Instructions

Our challenge lies in applying God's Word to our lives each second of living, resisting the temptations and trials that entice us to follow other ideologies and instincts.

Wonderful resources are available to help us apply godly wisdom to our lives. We need to be members of a Bible-teaching church, firmly rooted in a temple that teaches the truisms of the Bible. We should be part of a Christian fellowship of friends, people who help hold us accountable by reinforcing God's Word through conversation and comradery (see Hebrews 10:24–25).

Putting in practical boundaries that limit our exposure to things that may tempt us works well as we endeavor to follow God's precepts. Being mindful of the people we associate with helps us to avoid absorbing anti-Christian philosophies and passions. Monitoring and restricting our time spent with secular media, the people we associate with, the books we read, what we listen to, and the movies we see, significantly helps in our quest to quash unrighteous desires. Many of our sinful desires arrive through the things we see, read, and hear, motivating us to use our talents and gifts to satisfy selfish desires, such as using our education to earn money for fancy cars, sexual conquests, or vacation homes, instead of using our abilities and gifts to store up treasures in heaven through righteously serving others (see 1 John 2:15–17).

Placing a priority on spending time alone with God for prayer and Bible study equips us to follow the teachings of Jesus. As people selling righteously, our most important appointment remains the meeting with God each day. Setting aside quality time for this meeting every day helps greatly as we attempt to grasp the specifics of God's guidance for our lives. The Bible contains numerous places where Jesus spent time alone with God.

Be a Dedicated Prayer Warrior

If we believe God exists, then we also believe that He is someone who we want to constantly communicate with. This translates into an active prayer life, one in which we pray about everything and worry about nothing. To be a prayer warrior doesn't mean we have to spend two consecutive hours in prayer, but we should rarely let two hours go by without communicating with God, even it's only a brief "Lord help me" or a "Thank you, God" message.

In the book of Matthew, Jesus gives everyone a pattern of prayer to emulate. In Jesus's example, He advocates praying in a private place, alone with God. He begins the prayer by acknowledging who God is and His desire for God's will to be done. The prayer includes praise, a request for protection, and a plea for forgiveness of sins. We can find a private place to pray anywhere; it doesn't have to be at home or church. We can pray in a car, cubicle, or conference room. The Bible says we should pray without ceasing. We should humble ourselves to pray before and after meetings and before and after discussing sales strategy with a superior. In prayer, we can ask God how to handle objections, ask questions, and close sales (see Matthew 6:5–13 and 1 Thessalonians 5:17).

Pray, Pray, and Pray Again

To be a prayer warrior doesn't mean we have to spend two consecutive hours in prayer, but we should rarely let two hours go by without praying, communicating with God.

The book of James says that the prayers of a righteous person are powerful and effective. An important part of prayer involves listening so we can be obedient to God's instructions. God speaks to us in various ways; our challenge lies in being able to discern the voice of God, the voice of His Holy Spirit. We must learn how to sense the voice of His Holy Spirit and be sensitive and obedient to His voice. The best way to verify if what we hear is coming from the Holy Spirit is through the Bible, His written Word. The Bible will confirm what we believe and hear in prayer; it will not contradict any biblical precepts. In 1 John, the Apostle John says the Spirit must acknowledge that Jesus Christ has come in the flesh to be God's Spirit. This means the words we hear and the instructions we receive in prayer must be in concert with the teachings of Jesus.

For example, if we pray for wisdom in overcoming an objection and someone gives us advice that advocates exaggerating benefits or presenting inaccurate research, then we know this is not God answering our prayers. The Bible says this type of spirit belongs to Satan, who roams the earth seeking believers to devour (see James 5:16 and 1 John 4:2–3).

Be a Director of Every Thought

We direct thoughts by intellectually capturing each notion and emotion, then managing where it should go and how it should be used. This means we view each idea or inclination from a godly perspective, making sure that what we are pondering or doing aligns with and is subservient to the teachings of Jesus Christ. For example, if we receive advice about prospecting, we must capture that information, analyze it in the light of God's Word, and then either discard those thoughts and actions and reject them with every encounter. Or we may save those thoughts and actions for righteous use at the right time. We must go through this process with each thought and emotion, regardless of how it originates. Ideas and inclinations can arrive through other people, circumstances, our own mind-observations, things, and even Satan.

As righteous sellers, even though we live in the world, we do not earn our wages in the same way the world does. We earn our wages through the resources God gives us to sell righteously. These resources always include our innate talents and spiritual gifts, along with other things like prayer, praise, and biblical application. We use these resources to demolish strongholds, arguments, and pretensions—anything that stands in opposition to doing things God's way. This allows us to earn wages and even become wealthy in ways that align with biblical wisdom. In the book of Deuteronomy, Moses tells us to remember it's God who gives us the ability to become wealthy. The Bible says we must use all these resources—the apostle Paul calls them weapons—to take captive every thought and make it obedient to Jesus Christ (see Deuteronomy 8:18 and 2 Corinthians 10:3–5).

Also, the advice from Jesus's disciple Peter works wonderfully as we direct our thoughts. He reminds us to speak in ways that use the words of God, and to serve in the strength God provides. By capturing thoughts and emotions and analyzing them from a biblical perspective before we say or do anything helps us to sell righteously (see 1 Peter 4:11).

Take Thoughts Captive

We direct thoughts by intellectually capturing each notion and emotion, then managing where it should go and how it should be used. This means that we view each idea or inclination from a godly perspective, making sure that what we are pondering or doing aligns with and is subservient to the teachings of Jesus Christ.

Be Dutifully Repentant

We all make mistakes. We do and say things that are unethical or sinful, which makes being repentant vital to selling righteously. Viewing repentance as a responsibility and consistently confessing sin means we should have a process for, and periods of, self-examination and repentance. Jesus's first instruction when He began preaching was to repent. The important thing is to accept and confess sin, then make every effort to eliminate the sin. This requires us to go through a process of examining and eradicating the motivation that led to sinning, calling out to God in truth, praying in unabashed honesty, and seeking God and His Holy Spirit to empower us to overcome our sin.

True repentance involves godly sorrow. Our sin should make us feel uncomfortable and convicted. This should be followed by an inspiration from the Holy Spirit to change our thinking and behavior. We should yearn to work with God to be rid of our sin, as we strive to thrive in the freedom, grace, and mercy of our Lord and Savior, Jesus Christ. If we continue using a selling style that accommodates sin, then we may get entangled in destructive habits that delay our earthly success. We are prone to commit sins that entangle us in negative consequences, so we must constantly guard against any ignorance or lack of conviction that allows our sinful behavior to become a sinful lifestyle. The Bible says that the Lord is patient and wants everyone to attain repentance (see Matthew 4:17 and 2 Peter 3:8–9).

Confession is also vital to any repentance process. If we confess our sins, God will purify us of all unrighteousness, but if we don't confess them, God's Word has no place in our lives. We cannot obtain all the blessings of selling God's way if we cling to sin, because sin separates us from God. Separation from God is dangerous; it's a disconnection that could close the door to God's blessings and open a door for Satan to shove hell into our lives.

For example, we cannot mistreat our spouse, cheat on taxes, or victimize coworkers and then expect God to reward our sales career. People who persist in sin, rejecting biblical truth, subject themselves to God's discipline and the disruption of their prayers. God can do miraculous things to help us. To receive the blessings of God, we need Him active in our lives, forgiving our sins and responding to our prayers. Only through God's grace and mercy can the Holy Spirit lead us to success (see Isaiah 59:1–2, Romans 2:7–8, and 1 John 1:9–10).

Be Diligent about Building God's Kingdom

As believers, we have an obligation to lead others into the kingdom of God that's offered through Jesus Christ. If we remain diligent in using biblical tools to sell and serve as many people as possible, then our work will serve as a testimony that leads others to follow God. Jesus commands us to go and make disciples throughout all the nations (see Matthew 28:19).

The Bible says it rains on the righteous and the unrighteous, and God causes His sun to rise on the good and the evil. As people who sell righteously, we will face difficulties and disappointments, such as sales slumps, career setbacks, and even demonic attacks. During these times, it may be difficult to sense the presence of God, making it tough to understand His timing and our own destiny—especially if the people around us appear to be enemies and the factors against us look overwhelming.

However, we must remain diligent in righteous behavior as we strive to sell successfully and not behave in ways contrary to godly wisdom. We must continue to show our love for God and others by selling righteously. Jesus said the two greatest commandments are to love God with all our heart, soul, and mind and to love others as we love ourselves. He even tells us to pray for those who persecute us. Trials and tribulations can cram worry and weariness into the time and places where prayer and praise should reside. Our love for God and others should serve as the motivation to sell righteously, propelling us to use the tools of faith to sell and serve as many people as possible.

A biblical proverb states that the sluggard craves and gets nothing, but the desires of the diligent are fully satisfied. The book of Hebrews promotes God's justice and promises that He will not forget our work and the love we have shown to Him and others. The Bible tells us to be diligent to the very end, to not become lazy, and to imitate those who through faith and patience inherited the promises of God (see Proverbs 13:4, Matthew 5:43–48, and Hebrews 6:10–12).

Sell and Serve

Our love for God and others should serve as the motivation to sell righteously, propelling us to use the tools of faith to sell and serve as many people as possible.

Be Decidedly Thankful

All that is worthwhile and wonderful comes from God. Love, joy, peace, patience, kindness, goodness, faithfulness, gentleness, self-control, grace, mercy, wisdom, the Holy Spirit, and the ability to earn wealth come from our Father in Heaven. The most important thing we should be thankful for is clearly displayed in John 3:16, which says, "*God so loved the world that he gave his one and only son, that whoever believes in him shall not perish but have eternal life.*" Jesus's horrific death on the cross served as the atoning sacrifice for our sins, not just for our sins, but the sins of everyone we know and love.

Jesus's sacrifice assures us that apart from anything we experience on earth, our souls remain destined to dwell eternally in paradise. The book of Revelation tells us that there will be a never-ending time when God lives with us and that death, sorrow, woeful crying, and pain will all be gone forever. There is no accurate comparison between the possible hundred years that we could live in this world and the infinite years we will live in Heaven because of God's great love for us. This should make it easier to remain thankful in all circumstances. We should extend gratitude to God in humility and honor, thankful for all the goodness and blessings that we experience (see Revelation 21:3–4 and 1 Thessalonians 5:18).

Fully Commit to Selling Righteously

In the Introduction, I stated that whatever way you sell now expresses your faith. It reveals your god—that is, what you rely on for significance, security, and success. Now, I ask you to fully commit to selling God's way, totally relying on the Holy Spirit to sell righteously, as you commit to living a Christ-centered life. You have a choice and a free will to follow whatever god you desire, but remember that without the choices that Jesus made, we would have no choice. Jesus said that we did not choose Him, but that He chose us. His choice to serve us through an obedient, sacrificial life on earth, followed by a terrifying death on the cross, gave us all a choice. We can now choose our own path and providence (see John 15:16).

Let's not forsake the advice of the Apostle Paul, who beseeches us to join him and others in following the pattern that God gave us. In Philippians chapter 3, he writes with tears in his eyes that many live as enemies of Jesus. Their destiny is destruction; "*their god is their stomach*," which means their god is their appetite, and they glorify things they should be ashamed of; their minds are on earthly things. But our citizenship is in Heaven, where Jesus transforms our lowly bodies into glorious bodies like His own (see Philippians 3:17–21).

In the final chapter of the book of Joshua, after the Israelites wandered through the desert for forty years and finally arrived at the Promised Land, their leaders gathered everyone together, and Joshua spoke. He asked them to fear the Lord and serve God faithfully. He asked them to discard the gods and things their forefathers followed. He gave them a choice, saying if serving the Lord was undesirable, then they should choose which gods they would serve. But Joshua said, "*For me and my house, we will serve the Lord*" (see Joshua 24:14–15).

Question

If selling God's way and serving the Lord is undesirable, then choose today which gods you will serve. Will it be the Bible's God, money, greed, or some other self-serving ambition?

Scriptural References

- Far too many people follow a path to hell by selling in ways that accommodate sin:

  For of this you can be sure: No immoral, impure or greedy person—such a person is an idolater—has any inheritance in the kingdom of Christ and of God (Ephesians 5:5).

- God alone is sovereign:

  And God spoke all these words: "I am the Lord *your God, who brought you out of Egypt, out of the land of slavery. You shall have no other gods before me"* (Exodus 20:1–3).

- Without faith, it is impossible to please God. He rewards those who sincerely seek Him:

  And without faith it is impossible to please God, because anyone who comes to him must believe that he exists and that he rewards those who earnestly seek him (Hebrews 11:6).

- No one can serve two masters. We cannot serve both God and money. I wonder if most salespeople devote more time to selling rather than to serving God:

  No one can serve two masters. Either you will hate the one and love the other, or you will be devoted to the one and despise the other. You cannot serve both God and money (Matthew 6:24).

- If we change and humble ourselves before God, surrendering all areas of our life to Him, we will be lifted up:

Come near to God and he will come near to you. Wash your hands, you sinners, and purify your hearts, you double-minded. Grieve, mourn and wail. Change your laughter to mourning and your joy to gloom. Humble yourselves before the Lord, and he will lift you up (James 4:8–10).

- We must be doers of the Word and not just hearers. We need to apply biblical wisdom to all aspects of our lives. For this, we will be blessed:

  Do not merely listen to the word, and so deceive yourselves. Do what it says. Anyone who listens to the word but does not do what it says is like someone who looks at his face in a mirror and, after looking at himself, goes away and immediately forgets what he looks like. But whoever looks intently into the perfect law that gives freedom, and continues in it, not forgetting what they have heard, but doing it—they will be blessed in what they do (James 1:22–25).

- We need to be firmly rooted in a Bible-teaching church, passionately participating in praise, prayer, worship, ministries, giving, classes, community outreach, and Christian fellowship:

  And let us consider how we may spur one another on toward love and good deeds, not giving up meeting together, as some are in the habit of doing, but encouraging one another—and all the more as you see the Day approaching (Hebrews 10:24–25).

- Much of the sin in our lives comes through our own evil desires, brought about by the worldly things we see, read, and hear:

  Do not love the world or anything in the world. If anyone loves the world, the love of the Father is not in him. For everything in the world—the lust of the flesh, the lust of the eyes, and the pride of life—comes not from the Father but from the world. The world and its desires pass away, but the man who does the will of God lives forever (1 John 2:15–17).

- Jesus gives everyone a pattern of prayer to emulate:

  And when you pray, do not be like the hypocrites, for they love to pray standing in the synagogues and on the street corners to be seen by others. I tell you the truth, they have received their reward in full. But when you pray, go into your room, close the door and pray to your Father, who is unseen. Then your Father, who sees what is done in secret, will reward you. And when you pray, do not keep on babbling like pagans, for they think they will be heard because of their many words. Do not be like them, for your Father knows what you need before you ask him.

  This, then, is how you should pray: "Our Father in heaven, hallowed be your name, your kingdom come, your will be done on earth as it is in heaven. Give us today our daily bread. And forgive us our debts, as we also have forgiven our debtors. And lead us not into temptation, but deliver us from the evil one" (Matthew 6:5–13).

- We should pray without ceasing:

  Pray continually (1 Thessalonians 5:17).

- Prayer can be powerful and effective:

  Therefore confess your sins to each other and pray for each other so that you may be healed. The prayer of a righteous man is powerful and effective (James 5:16).

- An important part of prayer involves listening and observing so that we can verify that what we receive comes from God. What we receive must not dispute but support the teaching of Jesus:

  This is how you can recognize the Spirit of God: Every spirit that acknowledges that Jesus Christ has come in the flesh is from God, but every spirit that does not acknowledge Jesus is not from God. This is the spirit of the antichrist, which you have heard is coming and even now is already in the world (1 John 4:2–3).

- Moses reminds us that it's God who gives us the ability to become wealthy:

  But remember the LORD your God, for it is he who gives you the ability to produce wealth, and so confirms his covenant, which he swore to your ancestors, as it is today (Deuteronomy 8:18).

- Taking your thoughts captive helps demolish strongholds, arguments, and ideas that oppose godly wisdom:

For though we live in the world, we do not wage war as the world does. The weapons we fight with are not the weapons of the world. On the contrary, they have divine power to demolish strongholds. We demolish arguments and every pretension that sets itself up against the knowledge of God, and we take captive every thought to make it obedient to Christ (2 Corinthians 10:3–5).

- Peter's instructions work wonderfully as we capture thoughts and direct behavior:

If anyone speaks, they should do it as one speaking the very words of God. If anyone serves, they should do so with the strength God provides, so that in all things God may be praised through Jesus Christ. To him be the glory and the power forever and ever. Amen. (1 Peter 4:11).

- Being repentant is vital to selling righteously. Jesus's first instruction when He began preaching was to repent:

From that time on Jesus began to preach, "Repent, for the kingdom of heaven has come near" (Matthew 4:17).

- God is patient and wants us all to attain repentance. God does not want any of us to perish:

But do not forget this one thing, dear friends: With the Lord a day is like a thousand years, and a thousand years are like a day. The Lord is not slow in keeping his promise, as some understand slowness. Instead he is patient with you, not wanting anyone to perish, but everyone to come to repentance (2 Peter 3:8–9).

- Sin separates us from God. People who persist in sin, rejecting biblical truth, subject themselves to God's discipline and the disruption of their prayers:

  Surely the arm of the LORD is not too short to save, nor his ear too dull to hear. But your iniquities have separated you from your God; your sins have hidden his face from you, so that he will not hear (Isaiah 59:1–2).

  To those who by persistence in doing good seek glory, honor and immortality, he will give eternal life. But for those who are self-seeking and who reject the truth and follow evil, there will be wrath and anger (Romans 2:7–8).

- If we confess our sins, God will purify us of all unrighteousness, but if we don't confess our sins, God's Word has no place in our lives:

  If we confess our sins, he is faithful and just and will forgive us our sins and purify us from all unrighteousness. If we claim we have not sinned, we make him out to be a liar and his word has no place in our lives (1 John 1:9–10).

- Being diligent in our efforts to love God and others will lead us to sell successfully:

  The sluggard's appetite is never filled, but the desires of the diligent are fully satisfied (Proverbs 13:4).

- Regardless of people and circumstances, we must continue to sell righteously:

You have heard that it was said, "Love your neighbor and hate your enemy." But I tell you: Love your enemies and pray for those who persecute you, that you may be sons of your Father in heaven. He causes his sun to rise on the evil and the good, and sends rain on the righteous and the unrighteous. If you love those who love you, what reward will you get? Are not even the tax collectors doing that? And if you greet only your own people, what are you doing more than others? Do not even pagans do that? Be perfect, therefore, as your heavenly Father is perfect (Matthew 5:43–48).

- The wisdom of the Bible tells us to be diligent to the very end. God is just, and He will not forget our work and the love we have shown to Him and others:

  God is not unjust; he will not forget your work and the love you have shown him as you have helped his people and continue to help them. We want each of you to show this same diligence to the very end, so that what you hope for may be fully realized. We do not want you to become lazy, but to imitate those who through faith and patience inherit what has been promised (Hebrews 6:10–12).

- Heaven is a place where death, sorrow, and pain no longer exist; it's a place prepared for the people of God:

  And I heard a loud voice from the throne saying, "Look! God's dwelling place is now among the people, and he will dwell with them. They will be his people, and God himself will be with them and be their God. 'He will wipe every tear from their eyes. There will be no more death' or mourning or crying or pain, for the old order of things has passed away" (Revelation 21:3–4).

- Be committed to being thankful, decide to find something to be grateful for in all circumstances:

  Give thanks in all circumstances; for this is God's will for you in Christ Jesus (1 Thessalonians 5:18).

- Jesus's choice to serve us through an obedient, sacrificial life on earth, followed by a terrifying death on the cross, gave us all a choice. We can choose our own path and providence. However, without Jesus's choice, we would have no choice:

  You did not choose me, but I chose you and appointed you to go and bear fruit—fruit that will last—and so that whatever you ask in my name the Father will give you (John 15:16).

- The Apostle Paul beseeches us to join him and others in following the pattern that God gave us:

  Join together in following my example, brothers and sisters and just as you have us as a model, keep your eyes on those who live as we do. For, as I have often told you before and now say again even with tears, many live as enemies of the cross of Christ. Their destiny is destruction, their god is their stomach, and their glory is in their shame. Their mind is on earthly things. But our citizenship is in heaven. And we eagerly await a Savior from there, the Lord Jesus Christ, who, by the power that enables him to bring everything under his control, will transform our lowly bodies so that they will be like his glorious body (Philippians 3:17–21).

- If selling God's way and serving the Lord is undesirable, then choose today which gods you will serve. In the final chapter of the book of Joshua, after the Israelites wandered through the desert for forty years and then finally arrived at the Promised Land, their leaders gathered everyone together, and Joshua spoke:

  Now fear the Lord and serve him with all faithfulness. Throw away the gods your ancestors worshiped beyond the Euphrates River and in Egypt, and serve the Lord. But if serving the Lord seems undesirable to you, then choose for yourselves this day whom you will serve, whether the gods your ancestors served beyond the Euphrates, or the gods of the Amorites, in whose land you are living. But as for me and my household, we will serve the Lord (Joshua 24:14–15).

APPENDIX:

Seven Characteristics of Powerful Sales Presentations

All presentations should arise out of previously gathered information, offer a way to solve problems or maximize opportunities, and include a vision of the future with the proposed solution in place. These are the three core components of any sales presentation. For salespeople selling righteously, our powerful presentations should also include all seven of the characteristics that were discussed in chapter 7 as a way of using biblical principles in business presentations:

1. *The presentation should take place somewhere that serves as our "sacred" selling ground.* This is a place we can also pray about because we want it to help illuminate what we sell and reinforce the credibility of what we say. It could be our office, conference room, or retail selling floor. We should also use technology, displays, or signage to create a sacred selling space if our selling style requires mobility. God delivers the burning bush presentation in a place that He tells Moses is holy ground. In Luke 22, Jesus sends two disciples to prepare a large upper room. It's there that Jesus washes the disciples' feet and presents life-changing information (see Exodus 3:5 and Luke 22:10–12).

2. *Something in our presentation should attract attention and gather momentum.* This may be a demonstration, question, statement, or even an unexpected way of communicating or displaying our information. But it must be presented in a way that clears the prospect's mind of any distractions, allowing the prospect to focus on what we sell, intellectualize its importance, and stay attentive throughout our entire presentation. God uses a burning bush to capture Moses's attention. As a symbolic way to emphasize the importance of what he is saying, Jesus Christ attracts attention by washing His disciples' feet (see Exodus 3:2–3 and John 13:12).
3. *Somewhere in the presentation, we should identify ourselves in a way that allows the prospect to comprehend our capabilities, resources, and accomplishments.* Prospects need to know what we're capable of accomplishing and how we get things done. At times, we may need to highlight past achievements or use client testimonials to verify our claims. But we need prospects to understand our ability to serve, along with our power to provide solutions and opportunities. In the burning bush presentation, God identifies Himself to Moses, saying, "*I am the God of your father, the God of Abraham, the God of Isaac and the God of Jacob.*" After washing their feet, Jesus tells his disciples that they are correct in calling him "Teacher" and "Lord," for that is who He is (see Exodus 3:6 and John 13:13).
4. *The presentation should include a detailed description of the problem we're addressing or a detailed description of the*

opportunity for which we are advocating. Featuring the problem or opportunity in detail within the presentation demonstrates that we fully understand the prospect's situation, that we can provide a solution that's in their best interest in a time frame that's connected to some sense of urgency. In the burning bush presentation, God says, "*I have indeed seen the misery of my people in Egypt. I have heard them crying out because of their slave drivers, and I am concerned about their suffering.*" John 13 says that Jesus knows the time has come for Him to leave this world, and not coincidentally, He wants the disciples to know that this provides them a great opportunity to love and serve others (see Exodus 3:7, John 13:3, and John 13:12).

5. *We need to give prospects specific instructions during our presentations.* A prospect needs to know exactly what to do after our presentation ends. This paves the way for the sales process to end successfully, without any confusion or dissension. It also allows integrity to flow through the presentation because it confirms that we have no hidden agendas or questionable ambitions. Finally, including the instructions about how to proceed after the presentation ends provides the prospect with an opportunity to air any objections they or others may have. In Exodus 3, God instructs Moses to bring His people the Israelites out of Egypt. After washing the disciples' feet, Jesus instructs them to make others clean in the same way that He has made them clean (see Exodus 3:10 and John 13:14–15).

6. *Questions from the prospect should be part of our presentations.* Questions interjected in our presentation from prospects indicate either a rising level of interest or a lack of clarity regarding what we're selling. So, these questions give us an opportunity to either clear up confusion or expound upon the benefits of what we offer. What we don't need is the absence of questions from prospects during our presentations because that would indicate a significant lack of interest. Moses shows significant interest in what God presents to him when he asks, "*Who am I, that I should go to Pharaoh and bring the Israelites out of Egypt?*" The disciple Peter's interest is so keen as Jesus washes other disciples' feet that he asks if he is going to get his feet washed as well (see Exodus 3:11 and John 13:6).
7. *Guarantees need to be a major part of our sales presentations.* We need to guarantee as many aspects of our product or service as possible, even if it's just a promise to refund the cost or replace what was sold if needed. We should also guarantee righteous things that we feel personally committed to delivering, like a commitment to being honest, accessible, and respectful. Of course, our most important guarantees revolve around our product's ability to deliver the features and benefits presented. The Lord delivers His guarantee when He tells Moses, "*I will be with you.*" Jesus guarantees His disciples a sacred gift when He states, "*Now that you know these things, you will be blessed if you do them*" (see Exodus 3:12 and John 13:17).

Scriptural References

- Our sales presentation needs to take place somewhere that serves as our "sacred" selling ground. This is a place that illuminates what we offer while reinforcing the credibility of what we communicate:

  "Do not come any closer," God said. "Take off your sandals, for the place where you are standing is holy ground" (Exodus 3:5).

  He replied, "As you enter the city, a man carrying a jar of water will meet you. Follow him to the house that he enters, and say to the owner of the house, 'The Teacher asks: Where is the guest room, where I may eat the Passover with my disciples?' He will show you a large room upstairs, all furnished. Make preparations there" (Luke 22:10–12).

- Something in our presentation should attract attention and keep the focus on what we are selling. God uses a burning bush to capture Moses's focus and Jesus attracts attention by washing His disciples' feet:

  So Moses thought, "I will go over and see this strange sight—why the bush does not burn up" (Exodus 3:3).

  When he had finished washing their feet, he put on his clothes and returned to his place. "Do you understand what I have done for you?" he asked them (John 13:12).

- Somewhere in our presentations, we should identify ourselves in a way that allows the prospect to conceptualize our capabilities, resources, and accomplishments. God identifies Himself to Moses as the God of his father; Jesus tells his disciples that they are correct in calling him "Teacher" and "Lord."

  Then he said, "I am the God of your father, the God of Abraham, the God of Isaac and the God of Jacob." At this, Moses hid his face, because he was afraid to look at God (Exodus 3:6).

  "You call me 'Teacher' and 'Lord,' and rightly so, for that is what I am" (John 13:13).

- The presentation should include a detailed description of the problem or the opportunity we're addressing:

  The LORD said, "I have indeed seen the misery of my people in Egypt. I have heard them crying out because of their slave drivers, and I am concerned about their suffering" (Exodus 3:7).

  Jesus knew that the Father had put all things under his power, and that he had come from God and was returning to God (John 13:3).

  When he had finished washing their feet, he put on his clothes and returned to his place. "Do you understand what I have done for you?" he asked them (John 13:12).

- We need to give prospects specific instructions during our presentations. Prospects need to know every detail of what they must do to purchase our product:

  So now, go. I am sending you to Pharaoh to bring my people the Israelites out of Egypt (Exodus 3:10).

  Now that I, your Lord and Teacher, have washed your feet, you also should wash one another's feet. I have set you an example that you should do as I have done for you (John 13:14–15).

- Questions from the prospect should be part of our presentations. During a presentation, we need the prospect's attention, interest, and participation:

  But Moses said to God, "Who am I that I should go to Pharaoh and bring the Israelites out of Egypt" (Exodus 3:11)?

  He came to Simon Peter, who said to him, "Lord, are you going to wash my feet" (John 13:6)?

- Guarantees need to be a major part of our sales presentations. Our guarantees confirm the reliability of what we sell and the veracity of how we are selling it:

  And God said, "I will be with you. And this will be the sign to you that it is I who have sent you: When you have brought the people out of Egypt, you will worship God on this mountain" (Exodus 3:12).

  Now that you know these things, you will be blessed if you do them (John 13:17).

A Seller's Prayer

Dear Father in Heaven, Creator of the universe, I humble myself before You, faithfully believing that You are all-wise and loving. Almighty God, I desperately need You. Please lead and bless me as I strive to sell according to Your principles and precepts. Allow me a success and prosperity that yields to Your purpose for my life.

Dear Lord, forgive my sins as I forgive those who sinned against me. Please protect me from all that is evil and diabolical. It is only through Your grace and mercy that I can accomplish anything worthwhile. Teach me and lead me to remain in Jesus so that He can remain in me, supervising my thoughts, managing my emotions, and directing my behavior. Allow the Holy Spirit to guide me through every task.

Let my numbers be consistently fantastic. Allow me greatness in serving others. Let my relationships be complete in love and righteousness. Let me live according to Your Word, content with Your will, loving You as God, and loving others as Jesus taught.

Father, Your Word says in Revelation 13:11–18 that there will come a day when everyone will be forced to receive a mark on their right hand or forehead and that no one can buy or sell unless they have the mark, which is the name of the beast or the number of his name. Your Word says that this calls for wisdom and that if anyone has insight, let him calculate the number of the beast, because it's man's number. That number is 666. When that day comes, let those of us who seek and pray to You receive the wisdom and power to do things Your way, as it indicates in Revelation 20:4.

Thank You, dear God, for Your wonderful Holy Spirit, who serves as my Comforter and Counselor. Dear Jesus, I wait faithfully for Your return. I love You, Jesus, and remain eternally grateful for the way You served and sacrificed. All glory, praise, and honor belong to You, dear Father. It is in the matchless name of Jesus that I pray. Amen.

Scriptural References

- The Bible tells of a beast that will come out of the earth:

  Then I saw another beast, coming out of the earth. He had two horns like a lamb, but he spoke like a dragon. He exercised all the authority of the first beast on his behalf, and made the earth and its inhabitants worship the first beast, whose fatal wound had been healed. And it performed great and miraculous signs, even causing fire to come down from heaven to earth in full view of the people. Because of the signs it was given power to do on behalf of the first beast, it deceived the inhabitants of the earth. It ordered them to set up an image in honor of the beast who was wounded by the sword and yet lived. The second beast was given power to give breath to the image of the first beast, so that it could speak and cause all who refused to worship the image to be killed. It also forced everyone, small and great, rich and poor, free and slave, to receive a mark on their right hands or on their foreheads, so that no one could buy or sell unless they had the mark, which is the name of the beast or the number of his name. This calls for wisdom. If anyone has insight, let him calculate the number of the beast, for it is the number of a man. That number is 666 (Revelation 13:11–18).

- Christians who do not worship the beast will reign with Jesus for a thousand years:

  I saw thrones on which were seated those who had been given authority to judge. And I saw the souls of those who had been beheaded because of their testimony for Jesus and because of the word of God. They had not worshiped the beast or its image and had not received its mark on their foreheads or their hands. They came to life and reigned with Christ a thousand years (Revelation 20:4).

Acknowledgments

Obviously, most of the source material comes from the Holy Bible and my experiences. However, I must acknowledge the First Baptist Church of Glenarden in Prince George's County, Maryland, which I joined during the first part of 2004. The church, led by Pastor John K. Jenkins Sr, teaches biblical truth with clarity and tenacity; it is a devout Bible-teaching church and steadfast house of prayer. Pastor Jenkins is an outstanding teacher, leader, and humble disciple of Jesus Christ.

At the First Baptist Church of Glenarden, I have participated in several men's small groups, found numerous ways to serve others in my community, and taken classes to further my spiritual growth and commitment to follow Jesus. Any wisdom this book bestows is just a snippet of what I learned to at this Bible-teaching, Holy Spirit-filled church. I encourage anyone, regardless of religious beliefs, to attend one of the Sunday services at the First Baptist Church of Glenarden or view one of the services online on the church's website.

About the Author

Michael P. Hamer is a lifelong salesperson who began his sales career at age seven on the streets of Gary, Indiana, selling eggs with his deeply religious grandfather. During his college years, Michael spent a summer selling books door-to-door in Los Angeles. He also sold advertising space at a theater in Cambridge, Massachusetts, while in college.

Michael graduated from Boston University with a degree in communications, concentrating in advertising and marketing. After college, he spent almost thirty years in advertising sales in the radio and cable TV industries in the Washington, DC market. Michael held a variety of positions, from account executive to general sales manager, most notably with CBS Radio, Bonneville Broadcasting, and Media General. In his last media position, Michael served as a sales executive and manager with WAVA Radio, a Christian teaching and talk radio station.

Michael has received numerous awards and notable recognition for his sales and management accomplishments. Moved by the need for more transparency and accountability in corporate America, Michael promotes the return to time-honored ethical business practices in today's complex, evolving economy.

All glory, honor, and thanks go to God.

www.sellingGodsway.org

Finally, brothers and sisters, rejoice! Strive for full restoration, encourage one another, be of one mind, live in peace. And the God of love and peace will be with you.

—2 Corinthians 13:11

Endnotes

1. The Editors of *Encyclopaedia Britannica*, "The ServiceMaster Company," *Britannica Money*, accessed March 10, 2026, https://www.britannica.com/money/The-ServiceMaster-Company
2. *Tyson Foodservice*, "About Us — Core Values," accessed March 10, 2026, https://dev.tysonfoodservice.com/connect/about-us---core-values

www.ingramcontent.com/pod-product-compliance
Ingram Content Group UK Ltd.
Pitfield, Milton Keynes, MK11 3LW, UK
UKHW022002190726
13853UKWH00004B/1683